The Life and Times of
JAMES II

DVKE OF YORK

The Life and Times of
JAMES II

Peter Earle

Introduction by Antonia Fraser

Book Club Associates, London

*Series designed by Paul Watkins
Layout by Juanita Grout*

*Filmset by Keyspools, Golborne, Lancashire
Printed and bound in Great Britain by
Morrison and Gibb Ltd, London and Edinburgh*

Contents

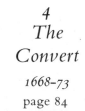

Introduction

PETER EARLE, in a stimulating new study, poses straight away the problem of James II to the biographer: his latter end, that sad Catholic flight from power in 1688, leading to the permanent establishment of the Protestant succession, has much bedevilled subsequent analyses of his reign, let alone of the man himself. To the Whig historians he has inevitably seemed a Papist villain, to the Catholics a heroic defender of the faith. It is thus particularly refreshing to be reminded that King James II – whose cause went down forever to Dutch William at the Battle of the Boyne – is after all one and the same person as the attractive James, Duke of York, the younger brother of Charles II, and one of the most appealing figures of the exiled Royalist entourage during the Civil War.

Somehow even James's appearance seems to have become blackened in the biased mirror of history: as a young man he was described as tall, fair and good-looking, in favourable contrast to his swarthy brother nicknamed the Black Boy. It was scarcely surprising that this agreeable, pleasant-mannered youth should have been the best-loved child of his mother, Queen Henrietta Maria. In the escapades of his early years, as deputy for his father at Hull at the beginning of the Civil War, or in his sensational getaway from the grasp of Parliament dressed as a woman, and still later as a soldier in the French army under Marshal Turenne, the picture that emerges is essentially an attractive one. In private life the youthful James not only enjoyed such traditionally royal pleasures as hunting with abandon, but acquired such a scandalous reputation with the ladies that he was described as 'the most unguarded ogler of his time' – it would have amazed a later age to have learnt that in the early 1660s the prowess of James in this respect was thought to equal that of his brother Charles. His most famous mistress, Arabella Churchill, was the sister of the future great Duke of Marlborough; and even his first marriage to Anne Hyde, daughter of his brother's Chancellor Clarendon, was directly occasioned by her pregnancy.

Such a picture of a royal younger brother, which has something in common with the style of the sons of George III, makes the results of James's conversion to Catholicism in 1668 seem all the more dramatic. For now all the courage and resolution which he had shown previously on the battlefield, on board ship as Lord High Admiral, in the hunting-field – or in the bedroom – were turned towards the proselytisation of the Catholic faith to which he gave his unstinted allegiance. And alas for his future on the English throne, each new twist of James's fortune showed how ill-equipped his nature was to cope with the immense demands such a course would make on even the most agile King in a resolutely Protestant country. His second marriage to a Catholic princess and the birth of a Catholic male heir may have been inevitable, but at the time they seemed to fit into the general pattern of disaster imposed by James. The trial of the seven bishops was the culmination of a process by which James, it appeared, was almost deliberately alienating the ruling class of Britain. In the throes of fighting off William, the husband of his Protestant daughter Mary, James was capable of making another mistake in fleeing, thus sacrificing his strong remaining prestige as King. So he came to spend the rest of his years in melancholy, if pious, exile in France, while his two daughters reigned in turn on his own throne.

Perhaps he lacked flexibility from the start, or perhaps over fifty years as a younger brother had fatally vitiated his original nature. In his own conclusion, however, Peter Earle aptly quotes the judgment of a lady of the French Court of the 1690s: '"King James was a brave and honest man," but unfortunately piety makes people outrageously stupid.' It is a cynical estimate perhaps, but one which the career of James II, from dashing young duke to melancholy exiled monarch, amply justifies.

Antonia Fraser

Acknowledgments

Photographs and illustrations were supplied by, or are reproduced by kind permission of the following. The pictures on pages 13/2, 18, 41, 49, 103/1, 103/2, *126–7*, 176, *190–1* are reproduced by gracious permission of H.M. the Queen; on page 59 by gracious permission of the Duke of Marlborough; on page 60 by kind permission of the Marquess of Bath; on page 58 by permission of the Earl of Chesterfield; on page *80 (below)* by permission of Earl Spencer; on page 100 (above and below) by permission of Viscount Hinchingbrooke; on pages *77 (above)* and 170 by permission of Lord Sackville; on page *178* by permission of Lt-Col R. Myddelton, Chirk Castle; on page 34 (right) by permission of Captain Berkeley, Berkeley Castle. Tom Annan: 68; Archives Photographiques: 37; Bibliothèque Nationale: 46–7; Denys E. Bower, Chiddingstone Castle: 85, 95, 159, 174, 181, 193, 212; BPC: *65/1, 114–15*; British Museum: 20–1, 26, 39, 54/1, 55/1, 82–3, 88/1, 89/1, 101, 104, 116–17, 138–9, 153, 155/1, 155/2, 172–3, 189, 202, 203, 210; Courtauld Institute of Art: 24; John Freeman: 116–17, 138–9; Giraudon: 36, 46–7; Guildhall Library: 160; N. Huddleston Esq: 136; Hudson's Bay Company: *65/1*, 71/2, 184; India Office Library: 70–1; A. F. Kersting: 122–3; George King: *77/1*, 170; London Museum: 54–5, 63/2, *80/1*; Longmans: *115/1*; Master and Fellows of Magdalene College, Cambridge: 62/2, 63/1; Mansell Collection: 34/1, 70/2, 106–7, 114/1, 120, 128–9, 154, 158, 171, 195, 196, 206–7, 208–9; Middle Temple: *65/2*; Musée Condé, Chantilly: 36; Musées Nationaux: 30–1, 38, 97; National Galleries of Scotland: *2*, 10–11, 40, *68*, 142/1, 142/2, 214, 215; National Maritime Museum: 73; National Monuments Record: 123/2; National Portrait Gallery: 13/1, 16, 25, 28, 35, 53, 62/1, 109, 143, 150, 156, *179*, 186; National Trust (Petworth): *14–15*; Radio Times Hulton Picture Library: 42, 198–9; Rijksmuseum, Amsterdam: 24, 78–9; Royal Academy: 56, 135, 166; Commissioners of the Royal Hospital, Chelsea: 145/1; Science Museum: 50–1, 66–7; Tom Scott: *2*; Rodney Todd-White: *80/1*, 145/1; Mrs P. A. Tritton, Parham Park: 88–9, 169; Château de Versailles: 30–1, 38, 97; Victoria and Albert Museum: *3*, 33, 77/2, 77/3, 90, 122/2, 145/2; Trustees of the Wallace Collection: 204–5; Jeremy Whitaker: *14–15*; Sir William Worsley: 91. Picture research by Jane Dorner.

1
A Stuart
Boyhood
1633-48

SOLDIER, SAILOR, failure, saint? James, Duke of York and Albany, later James II, is a puzzle to his biographer. Few people have written about him without emotion. Whig and latter-day Whig historians such as Macaulay, Trevelyan and Churchill have painted a black picture of the villain who tried to reimpose Popery on a Protestant nation. Catholic apologists have gone as far the other way in trying to whitewash him. But to the uncommitted, James is still an enigma. In his own lifetime his reputation soared up and down as violently as East India Company shares on the Amsterdam stock market. Now he was a national hero; a few months later the most hated man in England. Even a long, perspective view contains much ambiguity. Why should the man who was famous above all for his courage and resolution behave in such an apparently craven and irresolute way at the crisis of his life? We shall probably never know.

The story begins in the winter of 1628, when the English Court, always avid for novelty, was treated to a rare spectacle. The King and Queen were falling in love. A Court which had been forced to watch James I slobbering over his 'most humble Slave and Dogge, Steenie', otherwise known as George Villiers, Duke of Buckingham, had been alarmed to see the success with which the favourite had managed to transfer his ascendancy from the father to the son. Charles I seemed to be as much in Buckingham's power as his father had ever been, and treated his young wife, Henrietta Maria, sister to the King of France, with contempt. But the assassin's knife which cut Buckingham down in his prime was to make Henrietta 'not only the happiest princess, but the happiest woman in the world', for the King, grieving over the murder of his favourite, sought consolation and comfort in a place hitherto unexplored, the arms of his wife. What he found was certainly attractive. Small and neat like her husband, Henrietta Maria at nineteen had blossomed out into a real beauty – her affection and gaiety a marvellous foil to the King's melancholy and intense love of suffering. Twenty years later, when all her happiness had disappeared and she was mourning for the execution of her beloved husband, she could still be gay. Madame de Motteville, who met her in exile in Paris, tells us that 'even amid her tears, if it occurred to her to say something amusing, she would stop them to divert the

PREVIOUS PAGES One of the last portraits of Charles I, with James, Duke of York: painted by the school of Peter Lely.

12

company'. This gay, beautiful, chic and happy young Queen made many friends at Court, as she frittered away the quiet 1630s, followed by her train of dwarfs, negro servants, monkeys and dogs. But outside the small circle which shared her tastes, she was loathed. To begin with, she was far too French for the English, despite her fluent command of her husband's tongue. But much worse than being French, she was a Catholic, and made no secret of it. As such she was the victim of that terrifying and unreasoning hatred of Papists which will provide so much of the background to this book.

The royal love affair soon bore fruit. The first child, born prematurely, died soon after birth, but from 1630 onwards

ABOVE LEFT Henrietta Maria, by an unknown artist.
ABOVE RIGHT Portrait of Charles I, painted by Daniel Mytens in 1628. The view from the balustrade is believed to be of the Thames at Greenwich.

James, Duke of York, with his younger brother, Henry, Duke of Gloucester, and his youngest sister, Princess Elizabeth: painting by Peter Lely.

15

George Villiers, Duke of Buckingham – the great favourite of James I and Charles I – with his wife and family: portrait by Gerald Honthorst, 1628.

the royal nursery at St James's was always busy. Charles, Prince of Wales, was born in 1630, Mary in 1631, James, Duke of York, in 1633, Elizabeth in 1635. Then there was a period of temporary unemployment for the rockers of the royal cradle till Henry, Duke of Gloucester, was born in 1639. One last child, Henrietta, 'Minette', was born in very different circumstances in the middle of the Civil War. The royal children saw little of their parents, but the background of a successful marriage, and the general feeling of security and prosperity which characterised the 1630s, meant a happy family life for the growing children. The three eldest were brought up with the children of the murdered favourite, Buckingham, and passed their time between St James's and the royal palaces outside London – Hampton Court, Richmond and Greenwich.

James, a beautiful, fair, blue-eyed baby, was his mother's favourite. The newsletter announcing his birth on 14 October 1633 said he was a goodly, lusty child and reassured readers that the King and Queen were 'well and jolly'. A month after his birth, he was baptised at the chapel of St James's by the new

Archbishop of Canterbury, William Laud. There had been some criticism of the Queen's choice of his wet-nurse, a Catholic, no one knowing what a baby might take in with a Papist's milk, but no one could have quibbled with his god-parents, two of the most distinguished representatives of European Protestantism. His aunt Elizabeth, the widowed Queen of Bohemia, was the Queen of Hearts whose husband's struggle against the Catholic House of Habsburg had been the first cause of the Thirty Years' War, which was still denying peace to a shattered Europe. His godfather, Frederick Henry, Prince of Orange, was one of the heroes of that war, as he led the United Provinces in the last stages of their seemingly eternal struggle for independence against Spain. Almost a king in the republican Netherlands, he was to initiate that fateful alliance of the House of Orange with the royal House of Stuart. His son was to marry James's elder sister, Mary, and his grandson, William III, to marry another Mary, James's daughter. In 1633 all this lay well in the future, and public opinion, which welcomed the choice of godparents for the royal child, still bridled at the fact that Protestant England did nothing to aid the Protestant cause in Europe. Two peace-loving kings and a Catholic queen provided thin offerings for a nation still glorying in the memory of Elizabeth and war against Spain.

But the children playing in the royal nursery, or in the gardens of Hampton Court, cannot as yet have known much about that beast, public opinion. Happily oblivious of what the future offered, they played, learned to read and write, and worshipped God in a Protestant way. For Henrietta Maria, whose unbridled Papism made many converts at Court, was allowed no say in the chances of salvation of her own children. All except her last-born, Minette, who was raised in France, were brought up as staunch Protestants, and James and Charles received their first religious instruction not from their mother, but from their kindly and capable governess, the Protestant Countess of Dorset. This faith, well-taught and well-learned, was to remain unshaken until far into manhood.

The personalities of both James and Charles were to be affected for ever by the tragic events of the 1640s and the repeated disappointments of the 1650s, but, even as a child, James revealed much of the character which he was to retain as

a man. One key to his character lies in his relationship with his brother Charles. James was to be a younger brother for the first fifty-two years of his long life, and his release from the frustrations of playing second fiddle to a man he loved, but did not particularly admire, was to be a major cause of the disasters of his short reign as King of England. The brothers were very different. As a boy and a young man, James was the better-looking of the two, tall and fair with none of that cruelty about the mouth which characterises his later portraits. Charles was always dark, the 'Black Boy', the 'tall, black, man, two yards high' of the Parliamentary wanted notices. James as a child was gentler and more open-natured than his brother, though his good looks and pleasant manner concealed a powerful will and a stubbornness which were to grow stronger as he grew older. Although James was by no means stupid, he lacked the wit and wiliness which were so often to get his brother out of trouble. His mind worked on a single track, and he was incapable of appreciating the views of those who did not share that track. Wit, humour, the subtle nuances of a situation, all passed him by, and he was to be something of a social disaster in his brother's Court. But those who saw the two together in their youth often preferred the tall, fair, pleasant-mannered James.

Because the brothers were so different, and because it seemed to many to be in the nature of brothers to hate one another, there were often attempts to set them against each other. In a world of faction it seemed a natural thing to do. But such attempts rarely bore fruit. Charles often found James tiresome, but he never turned on him. As for James, a staunch monarchist by birth and inclination, he accepted without question the privileges of primogeniture. As God in His wisdom had created the institution of hereditary monarchy, so did He determine the order in which children should spring from a royal womb. James was always loyal to his brother, even though that brother never lived up to James's standards of leadership and determination. Indeed James felt that both his brother and his father had been far too soft with their opponents, and sometimes must have indulged in an unbrotherly wish that he, too, might be king, to show the world how a king should behave.

When James was still a very small child the problem of what was suitable behaviour for a king, which had lain dormant for

OPPOSITE James, Duke of York, at the age of eleven. This portrait by William Dobson was painted in Oxford, but left unfinished when the city surrendered to the Parliamentarians in 1646.

some years, became once more the dominant topic of conversation in the kingdom. Here is not the place to discuss in detail the extraordinarily complex origins of the Civil War, but it will be impossible to understand the later development of James's mentality unless we show the broad lines of the long struggle between King and Parliament which dominated the political history of England in the seventeenth century. A future regicide and republican, Edmund Ludlow, described the problem in famous words: 'The question in dispute between the King's party and us was, as I apprehended, whether the King should govern as a God by his will and the nation be governed by force like beasts; or whether the people should be governed by laws made by themselves, and live under a government derived from their own consent.' Most Stuart kings would have accepted this statement of the dispute, though they would have changed the wording a little. They did want to rule as gods by their will, and thoroughly approved the successful moves towards absolutism of their cousins on the Continent. But to do this they needed a plentiful supply of two closely-connected things – money and soldiers. As it was, they had neither, and therein lies their downfall. What other king in Europe could have found himself in the humiliating position of Charles I when he raised his standard at Nottingham, waiting, like a rebel himself, for loyal subjects to join him in subduing a revolt against his rule? Ironically, Charles found himself in this position as a result of his and his father's refusal to fight a war which many of his subjects would have fervently supported. The great Whig historian Macaulay makes the point with his usual gusto: 'Had James I been … a valiant, active and politic ruler, had he put himself at the head of the Protestants of Europe … and had he found himself, after great achievements, at the head of fifty thousand troops, brave, well disciplined, and devotedly attached to his person, the English Parliament would soon have been nothing more than a name.' Neither James I nor his son did this, and since they ruled an island apparently safe from the threat of invasion, they needed virtually no army. And even if they wanted to raise one, it was to Parliament that they must apply for the money. For the kings of England, so different from their cousins in France, had no right to initiate taxation without the consent of Parliament. And without taxation their

The House of Commons at Westminster in 1640, with drawings of the thirty-eight towns represented by that Parliament.

PLATFORM OF THE LOVVER HOUSE OF THIS PRESENT PARLIAMENT,

Assembled at *Westm*. : thirteenth day of *April, 1640*. and in the 17 Yeere of his Maiesties happie Raigne.

only major resource was the rapidly dwindling private income of the Crown. This might be supplemented in emergency by selling off Crown lands, but by 1640 there were few of these left. Parliament was only too aware of the King's financial weakness, and was determined to give its consent to new taxation only if the Stuart Kings qualified their desire to govern as gods.

Parliament itself bore little resemblance to the institution we know today. It was first and foremost an assembly of rich country gentlemen. Such as were also noblemen sat in the House of Lords, together with the bishops, themselves often the sons of country gentlemen. In the Lower House merchants and lawyers sat with the owners of country estates, but a little research into family history is sufficient to show that most of these too were the sons and brothers of country gentlemen, and that as soon as the law or trade had made them rich they also bought estates. The political opinions of these gentlemen ranged from fanatical support of hereditary monarchy to fanatical republicanism, but there were few who did not think that that accident of birth which distinguished them from the mass of their countrymen had made them fit to rule. When they talked about the right of the people to be governed by laws made by themselves, the people they referred to were property owners. What we in our wisdom call the people today were to them little more than beasts. Among this assembly of several hundred gentlemen were a few who trod a happy mean between the staunch monarchists to the right of them and the republicans to their left. Distinguished by their wealth as much as by their eloquence and leadership, they formed a middle party determined to destroy for ever the Stuart kings' desire for absolute monarchy, and to replace it by an oligarchy of property-owning Parliament men, ruling on behalf of all other property owners, and paying only lip-service and gentlemanly respect to that figurehead, a king. Half a century later, they appeared to have achieved their aim, but, for the moment, they discovered that they had stirred up more than they had intended – the whole ant-hill that was England. In the chaos that they created, a new sort of man often came to the fore, and the hitherto unsuspected aspirations of little men had to be heard and, when they had military power behind them, to be obeyed. Denzil Holles, a gentleman of the middle party, expressed the horror of his class when he remarked that 'the wisest of men saw it to be a great evil, that servants should ride on horses; an evil now seen and felt in this unhappy kingdom'.

The colours of the political spectrum were mirrored in an area of human speculation dear to the heart of seventeenth-century man – the correct path to salvation. Just as there was a left and a right in politics, so there was in religion. On the extreme right stood those still loyal to the Church of Rome. Moving to the left were to be met those who had reformed that Church, the more reformed the more to the left. Nearly in Rome itself, according to some critics, stood Archbishop Laud and his Arminians. Then came Anglicans who rejected the Archbishop's frills, next those who rejected bishops, and so on into the endless parade of Puritan sects which the chaotic times allowed to come into the open – Presbyterians, Independents, Baptists, Ranters and Fifth Monarchy Men. For a people who thought and spoke their politics in religious language, that beautiful language of King James's Bible, there was an obvious connection between religious and political belief. How could a Catholic be any other than a supporter of the most absolute of monarchies, if he was obliged to submit to that Antichrist the Pope? How could people who rejected all discipline and authority in religion be other than republican in politics? Here too there was a middle party – that essentially English compromise the Anglican Church, a Church for gentlemen who distrusted papal or episcopal authority as much as they despised the ranting of ill-educated mechanics. As the Civil War progressed, the middle party moved a little to the left, and Presbyterianism became its standpoint, but, once the troubles were over, they rejected such Calvinist and essentially un-English creeds to re-establish once again that Anglican dominance, the alliance of parson and squire which was to rule England in the eighteenth century.

A cleverer man than Charles I might have been able to control this turbulent England, but he, fumbling, disloyal to his friends and fundamentally dishonest, never had a chance. As for James, only eight at the beginning of the war, he can hardly have known much about what was going on, but he was to retain for ever a hardly surprising hatred for that insatiable and many-headed monster, Parliament. It was Parliament that

'The wisest of men saw it to be a great evil, that servants should ride on horses'

wrecked his happy home life, that drove his family out of London in the bleak January of 1642 to a Hampton Court whose shutters were closed, rooms icily cold and beds unaired. It was Parliament that drove his mother and his sister Mary, newly married to the young William of Orange, out of the country to try to raise money in Holland. And in April 1642, the young boy was to see what few boys like to see, the public humiliation of his father, the King. Charles, realising now that war against the Parliament was inevitable, was eager to secure possession of the royal arsenal at Hull. Doubtful of the loyalty of Sir John Hotham, the Governor, he made the rather foolish decision to send his young son James with a large body of courtiers to boost the wavering obedience of the Governor and citizens, on the pretence that they were making a purely social visit. James entered the city with his entourage, unannounced, as the country people were coming in for market day. The mayor gave them an official entertainment, but his and Hotham's suspicions of their behaviour were reinforced the next morning, when a letter arrived from the King stating his intention of dining with Hotham that day. Hotham gave orders

FAR LEFT James's eldest sister Mary, with her husband, William II of Orange, painted by Van Dyck. William died in 1650, a few weeks before the birth of his son and heir, who later became William III of England.

Sir John Hotham, the Governor of Hull, who closed the gates of the city against Charles I in 1642: silver medal by T. Simon, 1645.

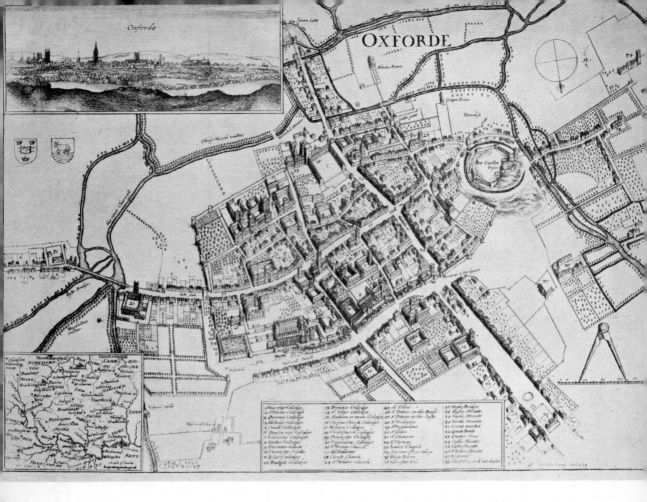

Oxford, which became the
Royalist headquarters
in 1642.

for the bridge to be drawn up, the gates shut and the guns
loaded, and when the King arrived he found the walls lined
with the train bands in their steel helmets. When the King
demanded to be let into his town, Hotham replied 'I dare not
open the gates to Your Majesty, since I am entrusted by the
Parliament with the safety of the town.' The King appealed to
the soldiers on the walls, but to no avail. He even had some
difficulty in persuading Hotham to release his son. The Civil
War had started. Years later, James, in his memoirs, was to
criticise both his father and his suite for the way in which they
had mishandled the situation. His solution was characteristically
blunt and straightforward: 'Some vigorous bold man should
have secured him [Hotham], or knocked him on the head.
Either would have done the work.'

James was too young to play any part in the Civil War, but
the lessons he learned during those impressionable early years

were fundamental to the make-up of his later character. They were quite different from the lessons learned by his brother Charles. James never outgrew the ultra-Royalism of the Cavaliers who first flocked to his father's standard. The royal cause was the right and only cause; there was no way of compromise. Those who opposed the royal will must be punished, and if necessary destroyed. Thirty years later, when his brother so artfully and cunningly fenced his way out of the great crisis of his reign, James once again would have used a bludgeon. Almost alone of his generation, James was not frightened of another Civil War to settle once again the arguments of politics.

James spent nearly all the Civil War in Oxford, the home of the Court and the Royalist headquarters after the King moved there in November 1642. The city of the Cavaliers must have been an exciting place for a young boy. During the early months of the struggle the Royalist gentry poured in, each vying to be more flamboyant, more courageous, more extravagant than the rest. They drank, swore, duelled and courted the ladies of the Court and town, while the town itself was turned into a fortified garrison. Magdalen College Grove became a gun park and New College Cloisters an arsenal. Other University buildings were used for storing food and other essential supplies. By the time that all the Cavalier volunteers and all the supplies needed to fight a war had been packed into the city, there was scarcely room to move, let alone to study. Many, indeed, who came up to study went out to fight. Anthony Wood, another boy who saw the war from Oxford and later wrote a history of the University, writes that some of the scholars 'were so besotted with the training and the activity and gaiety ... that they could never be brought to their books again. It was a great disturbance to the youth of the city.' These should have been important years in James's education, but it seems unlikely that he learned much from books in Cavalier Oxford. More likely he formed one of the crowd admiring the hero of the hour, his cousin Prince Rupert, or listening with joy to the bells and warming himself at the bonfires that greeted each Royalist victory, however small.

But, as the years passed, there were fewer bells. The soldiers who had cheered the early triumphs now marched by with their muskets reversed and their pikes dragging on the ground,

Algernon Percy, 10th Earl of Northumberland, who became warder to James and his younger brother and sister in 1646 after the surrender of Oxford: portrait after Van Dyck.

as yet another Cavalier hero was taken to his grave. Flamboyant dress began to look tatty, and high-spirited quarrels turned to bitter, sulky faction fights. King Charles was losing, and Oxford knew it. Prominent Royalists of the early days began to slink away to try to make a deal with Parliament while they still could. The King and the Prince of Wales continued to fight a depressing, losing war. James, alone of the royal family, remained in Oxford till the end in 1646, when the city surrendered to the army of Parliament. The Parliamentary officers treated the thirteen-year old boy well, 'for yet they had not banished all appearances of respect to the royal family'. Fairfax made 'a kind of speech' and Cromwell knelt to kiss the boy's hand. But when James went to London, despite his honourable escort, he knew he was a prisoner, parted from father, mother and elder brother – all alone.

James's prison was quite comfortable. It was, in fact, his old home, St James's Palace, and here he had the company of his young sister Elizabeth, who was to die a prisoner of Parliament, and his brother Henry, Duke of Gloucester. And Parliament could hardly have found a pleasanter warder than Algernon Percy, Earl of Northumberland, an old friend of his mother's and a very moderate Parliamentarian, of whom it was said 'no man had ever fewer idle words to answer for'. Northumberland was a sailor, and had commanded the ship-money fleet in 1636. Was it from his gaoler that James, the titular Lord High Admiral of England, got his first interest in the navy? It seems quite likely, but the main issue in James's mind was that he was a prisoner, and despite the very generous allowance voted him by Parliament, he was determined to escape. Such determination was strengthened by his father, whom he was allowed to see while he was held at Hampton Court, and by his mother, who insisted on sending him secret messages from Paris, which, when intercepted, made Parliament threaten to imprison him in the Tower. Two attempts at escape were checked but finally, after twenty months' imprisonment, his efforts were met with success. It was one of the few really successful things that he was to do in his life.

Every day James used to play hide and seek in the walled garden of the palace with his brother and sister. He had become so good at this, that often it was half an hour or longer before

28

he was found, and indeed his seekers often gave up the search. It was this period of half an hour that he used to escape. Locking up his sister's little dog, which had the habit of following him, he slipped out of a back door of which he had previously obtained the key. Here waiting for him was a gentleman for whom plots were the whole of life – Colonel Bampfield, a professional spy who later deserted the Royalist cause and, after many adventures, was taken on Cromwell's secret service payroll. Putting on a temporary disguise, James was taken by coach to a house near London Bridge, where Bampfield's confederate, the pretty Anne Murray, was waiting with girl's clothes. She had had some trouble with the tailor who had never seen a woman of James's shape, but the clothes were ready, and James cried 'Quickly, quickly, dress me.' In his new outfit, James then went to Billingsgate, where a barge which was waiting 'to take Mr Andrews and his sister' to Tilbury where a Dutch merchantman was cleared and ready to sail. Unfortunately, the bargemaster became suspicious when he saw Mr Andrews tying his sister's garter, and the latter plucking at her leg in a most unwomanish manner. Eventually he had to be taken into their confidence but, as luck would have it, he was a Royalist supporter and agreed to carry on with the flight as planned. To avoid the attention of the blockhouses at Gravesend, the barge sailed without lights as they slipped past on the evening tide, and so aboard the Dutchman. Here, if we can believe the hints of Madame de Motteville, who tells the story in her memoirs, James's troubles were of a different sort: 'As he was very handsome, the sailors suspected that he was not too virtuous.' Nonetheless, the voyage seems to have been fairly uneventful, except for a false alarm that they were being chased by an English frigate, and James stepped ashore at Middelburg in late April 1648, still wearing his girl's clothing. Some surprise was shown in the inn at the young gentlewoman who would not let the maids help her to bed, but James was safe. The Lord High Admiral had made his first voyage.

2
Soldier of
Fortune
1648-60

THERE IS SOMETHING intensely pathetic about the Cavaliers in exile. After the excitements of the Civil War and, for many, dramatic escapes from the clutches of Parliament, exile meant inevitable anti-climax and disillusion. Often with a price on their head, they were forced to stay amongst people who, after the first polite sympathy, soon became indifferent to their plight, if not downright hostile. Penniless, dressed in the tattered splendour of fashions soon to be ten years out of date, they hung about the ports of France, Holland and the Spanish Netherlands, or in the great cities of the hinterland, plotting, squabbling, intriguing and hoping, ever more hopelessly as the years went by, for some miracle to set them back in the fortunes they had so dearly lost. How tiresome they must have been, as they split up into increasingly bitter factions and spun unlikely stories to the courtiers in Paris and The Hague from whom they tried, usually unsuccessfully, to borrow money on the security of estates long since seized by Parliament. Nobody really loves a loser, and, after a few years, the English Court in exile at the Louvre or St Germain was reported to be little frequented by Frenchmen. Madame de Motteville tells us why: 'Their solitude is not surprising; ill-fortune was its cause; they had no favours to bestow. Theirs were crowns without power, which gave them no means of elevating men or of doing them benefits.' They were, in short, a dead loss.

It was into this miserable world that the fourteen-year-old James, still wearing his girl's clothes, descended in the late April of 1648. One of the first things he discovered was that in Europe, as in Oxford, he was still very much the younger brother. Soon after his arrival in the Netherlands, part of the Parliamentary fleet mutinied and James, encouraged by intriguers who reminded him that he was still Lord High Admiral of England, claimed the command of the only real power left in Royalist hands. Poor James; his bid for glory was thrust aside. Charles wanted to go and so Charles went. And thus it was to go on. Always Charles did the exciting things and James was left behind, often reduced to tears, as when Charles set off on his Scottish adventure which ended in the fiasco at Worcester. Indeed, Charles's adventures ended so often in disaster – disasters he would put to good account by his wittiness in describing them – that James must have felt justified in thinking he could have done better himself. There were many to encourage him. After all, with his father in the hands of Parliament and soon to be executed, and his brother risking his life in futile adventures, James, who was next in line, must have looked a good bet for the Crown. He was worth courting, and soon he found himself the focus for a set of intriguing Cavaliers who plotted and counterplotted against other Cavaliers who had gathered round Henrietta Maria in Paris or St Germain, or Charles himself.

They were for the most part a pretty miserable bunch; no match for Cromwell's spies who flitted around stirring up intrigue still further and reporting all back to their master in Whitehall. Closest to the Queen was Henry Jermyn, later Earl of St Albans, one of the few Cavaliers to become rich in France, a big sleepy man with 'an infinite capacity for intrigue but no other ability'. The man closest to James was Sir John Berkeley, a tough, self-assertive and tactless soldier, who was to be rewarded for his devotion to his master by a peerage, and later by the Lord Lieutenancy of Ireland – much to the amazement of his numerous detractors. Soon to join Berkeley at James's Court were his own and Jermyn's nephews. Charles Berkeley, later Earl of Falmouth, with as few brains as his uncle, had enormous charm and much loyalty and was a great favourite of both James and his brother. Harry Jermyn the younger was a tiny, affected man with a big head, whose success as a lady-killer was to astonish the Restoration gossip Grammont. Luckily for England, Charles himself attracted most of the talent: particularly that fat lawyer the Chancellor, Edward Hyde, a social-climbing snob with great ability and good sense; and the scheming Henry Bennet, later Earl of Arlington, who always wore a black plaster across the bridge of his nose to remind the world of the valour he had displayed when it had been broken at the skirmish of Andover. Bennet's edited face made him look sinister, if not romantic, and gave him a reputation for wit and incredible cleverness which he did not deserve, though he was a very competent linguist and diplomat.

All these men did well at the Restoration, but the truth was that in France there was really very little for all the intriguers to intrigue about. None of the royal family had any money to reward courtiers, nor did they have any jobs for them to do.

A cavalier in France playing the lute: an engraving of about 1640.

33

James's companions
in exile.
ABOVE Harry Jermyn the
younger, who became
Master of the Horse to
James at the Restoration,
and was later created
Lord Dover.
ABOVE RIGHT Sir John
Berkeley, later Lord
Berkeley of Stratton,
James's companion-
in-arms.
ABOVE FAR RIGHT
Henry Bennet, later
Earl of Arlington. He
always wore a black
plaster over the bridge of
his nose to commemorate
his valour in a skirmish
at Andover during the
Civil War.

All that was left was to try to intrigue each other out of the
positions of trust they held, to think up unlikely ways of
restoring the King or to try to find rich wives for the royal
brothers whose fortunes would serve to enrich them all. In
nearly all these matters they were totally unsuccessful. The
royal brothers, though both good-looking, were poor, and
rich heiresses of suitable rank felt it would be an unprofitable
employment of their fortunes to pour them out for the benefit
of the unfortunate House of Stuart.

In any case, the French had problems of their own. Louis XIII,
Henrietta Maria's brother, had died in 1643 and his successor,
Louis XIV, the future Sun King, was only five. France had a
habit of descending into anarchy or civil war when the king was
a minor, and this time was no exception. Opposition focussed
on the Queen Mother, the Spanish Anne of Austria, who had
established herself as regent, and her enormously clever but
devious minister, Cardinal Mazarin, a Sicilian of humble birth
whose previous occupations had included those of captain in
the Papal army and professional gambler. There were two main
groups of opponents to this rule by foreigners. On the one hand
were the Princes of the Blood Royal, furious at being excluded
from the power they felt to be their right and eager to plunder
what they could from a divided France. Their leaders were the
Prince de Condé, the impetuous, hawk-faced military hero of

34

the war still being waged against Spain, and the late King's brother, the ineffective Gaston of Orléans, whom a witty opponent described as having all that was necessary to make a fine gentleman, 'excepting courage'. Any deficiencies he may have had in this respect were more than made up by his extraordinary daughter, La Grande Mademoiselle, an Amazon of quite exceptional haughtiness whom it was suggested Charles should marry. Charles's wooing was inhibited by his real or pretended ignorance of French and La Grande Mademoiselle in fact preferred his brother James, whom she described as 'very pretty, with a good face and a fine figure. He spoke French well which made his manner more attractive than that of his brother.' But, in any case, the husband she was searching for was not likely to be a prince in exile.

The other centre of opposition to the Cardinal and the Queen Mother was the Parlement of Paris, an assembly of lawyers who normally had no real power, but now, bewitched perhaps by the success of their namesake across the Channel, claimed for themselves a law-making function to which they had no right. Although neither the Princes nor the Parlement were ever sufficiently united to do serious long-term harm to the French monarchy, Mazarin and the Queen Mother had some very awkward moments, and the first five years of James's exile in France were years of civil war, albeit a rather

Prince de Condé, military hero of the French war against Spain, who later went over to the enemy. In 1655 he was joined in the Spanish army by James, who had been ordered to leave France following Cromwell's treaty with Mazarin. Bust by Antoine Coysevox.

frivolous one. When he eventually joined his mother in February 1649, the Parisian mob had revolted and the city was being besieged by the royal army under Condé, not yet a rebel. A few days later a frightened French Court heard with horror the news of the execution of Charles I. It seemed a formidable warning to all kings of the weakness of their power and Madame de Motteville 'could not wonder enough at the evil influence that seemed to rule over those crowned heads, victims of the two parliaments of France and England'. The impression made on James, a boy of fifteen, by the murder of his father needs little emphasis, and it was probably at this time that he formed his resolution to become a soldier. To earn his living by the sword would solve the two main problems of the Cavalier in exile, boredom and shortage of cash, and at the same time the experience would befit him for the task of revenging himself on his father's murderers.

It was some time before James realised his ambition. He was still very young and it was to be three years before he persuaded his mother and his brother to let him go to fight. They were three frustrating years in which he was bandied about in the

36

Anne, daughter of Gaston of Orléans and first cousin to Louis XIV, known as La Grande Mademoiselle. Drawing by Mignard.

midst of Cavalier intrigue which seriously upset his relationships with both Charles and Henrietta Maria. The period was also broken by visits to Jersey, the last Royalist outpost, and to the Court of his lovely sister, Mary, at The Hague. It was here in January 1651 that he saw her little baby boy born a few weeks after the death of her husband. Fortunately James had no idea of the evil part that this infant nephew, William III of Orange, was to play in his life. Back in Paris James at last got his mother's permission to become a soldier. There remained only the problem of who to fight for. It was a familiar problem for Cavaliers who, sick of faction, chose to earn their living as soldiers of fortune. There were four main choices: to fight for the King of Spain against France, or the King of France against Spain, to join the army of the rebel Princes, now led by Condé, or to join the ranks of the freebooter Charles of Lorraine, always scheming and rarely fighting, of whom the great Marshal Turenne said, 'the promises of M. de Lorraine, and just nothing, are the same to me'. In the end, James, a grateful monarchist, decided to fight for the king whose country had sheltered his mother. He borrowed some money to buy his equipment, and

37

Marshal Turenne, James's
tutor in the art of war.
Turenne was the master
of manœuvre, taking
painstaking care and
calculating all his risks.
Drawing by Le Brun.

OPPOSITE Allegory of the
execution of Charles I.
The lopped oak represents
the fallen monarchy, from
which new shoots might
still grow – the three
exiled sons of the
dead King.

left Paris in the spring of 1652 to join the French royal army in
the company of Sir John Berkeley, who was to remain his
companion-in-arms.

James's years as a soldier were perhaps the happiest of his life.
A man at last, free from the disappointments and intrigue of
civil war and exile, free from the often unwelcome advice and
admonitions of his mother and brother, he was able to develop
talents hitherto dormant. Brave, obedient and loyal, quick to
grasp the essentials of a military situation, he soon earned by
merit the high rank in the French army fitting to his princely
station. In the numerous soldiers' memoirs of the 1650s, as
prolific and boring justifiers of their own importance then as
now, there is hardly a word of criticism for the young English
Prince earning his living as a soldier. James was no military
genius, but he was obviously a very good subordinate officer,
loved by his fellows and respected by his men. It is no wonder
that James, otherwise one of the most patriotic and nationalist
of English princes, should preserve a life-long affection for
things French.

His tutor in the art of war was the great Turenne, tutor to a
whole generation of soldiers, whose pupils included Louis XIV
and John Churchill, later Duke of Marlborough, as well as
James. The character and tactics of Turenne were in striking
contrast to the other French military genius of his age, the
Prince de Condé. Not for him the dash, the impetuosity, the
bad temper of his great rival. Turenne was the master of
manœuvre, the scientist who knew all the rules of seventeenth-
century warfare. Cautious, systematic, painstaking in his
appreciation of the ground, his risks were so well-calculated as
to be no longer risks, as he marched and countermarched,
advanced and retired in that great game of chess which was war.
James worshipped Turenne and learned well. His memoirs,
most certainly authentic for this period, are studded with praise
of his master, and full of examples of lessons learned. James
could be as brave as a lion, but thought little of pointless
heroism. In one action the Duke of Buckingham, another
Cavalier soldier of fortune, urges James to an impetuous action,
but James resists. 'I had no mind', he writes, 'to expose myself
to a certain defeat.'

James's memoirs of the wars reveal his character. Here

38

God exalteth y̒ low Tr—
—maketh thͤ dry Tre—
—to flourish Ezek:17:2—

Jan. 30. 1648

There is hope of a Tree if it be cut downe that it will Sprout
again and y̒ branches thereof will not cease though y̒ root of it wax
old in y̒ Earth and y̒ Stocke thereof be dead in y̒ Ground yet by the
Scent of Water it will bud and bring forth boughs Like a Plant
Job 14. 7. 8. 9.
done from y̒ Originall of Vaughan after the Murder of King Charles the First

RIGHT Mary,
Princess of Orange,
James's eldest sister.
Her Court at The Hague
became a refuge for the
royal exiles in the 1650s.

FAR RIGHT James Duke of
York, a portrait attributed
to Charles Wautier, and
probably painted when
James was serving with
the Spanish forces in
the Netherlands.

certainly is no great artist. Only occasionally are there the flashes
of cynicism and poetry that enliven so many memoirs of the
period. James writes in an earnest way, giving praise where it
seems to him to be due, sometimes becoming confused himself
in describing the confused campaigns in which he takes part.
Here we meet other French generals of the day, no match in
James's opinion for the great Turenne: the traitor Marshal
d'Hoquincourt who blackmails the French government into
paying him 20,000 crowns not to hand over the important
fortress of Péronne to the Spaniards; Turenne, not above
turning his coat himself, advises Mazarin to give him the
money: 'Once the Spaniards are in Péronne it will cost you
more than 20 millions, if not the loss of the kingdom'; the
courtier Marshal de la Ferté, not keen on fighting because his
influence at the Court depends on the number of men under his
command and dead men win no favours; the gallant mercenary
Count Schomberg, already in his mid-forties, who was to fight
for France, Holland, Portugal and Brandenburg before he lost
his life facing James across the River Boyne at the age of eighty-
two. These are the men who fill James's pages as the wars go on.

An Old ENGLISH MUSKETEER *with his Match Lock, Bandileers and Rest.*

What were these wars? When James first joined the royal army it was short of men and fighting the last stages of what seemed to be a desperate civil war against the rebel Princes. The highlight of this period and one of the most extraordinary battles of the epoch was the Battle of the Faubourg St Antoine, fought right underneath the walls of Paris on a hot July day in 1652. Condé, outmanœuvred by Turenne, marched for Paris in a last desperate effort to seize the city, but found the citizens now hostile to his cause, tired of war and refusing to open the gates. Condé was trapped in the suburb of St Antoine as Turenne marched up, and prepared to sell his life dearly behind the barricades in the narrow streets. Eager to watch the destruction of so valiant a gladiator were the citizens of Paris lining the walls, and the young King and his Court with a grandstand view from a hill outside the city. Turenne, always cautious and with time on his side, wanted to wait for the arrival of De la Ferté and the artillery, but the Court wanted action and ordered him to fight. And what a fight! Every wall and every street was defended with vigour. Condé himself, like a man possessed, was to be seen in twelve places at once, so hot inside his armour that at one time he stripped and rolled naked in a field in the suburb, 'as horses do'. Slowly he was forced back, ever more rapidly as De la Ferté arrived and the cannon started pounding. Surely this was to be the end of the great Condé? But no! Within the walls La Grande Mademoiselle had taken charge. The mayor was persuaded to open the gates and the young Amazon herself went to the Bastille to order the guns to fire on the royal army over Condé's head. Condé was safe, though the cause of the Princes was lost. And Mademoiselle? She was never forgiven. There was to be no king or emperor as a husband for her now.

Rarely were James's wars as exciting as this. Condé eventually changed his role from rebel to traitor and took his men over to the pay of the King of Spain. For the rest of the 1650s James was to fight in the last campaigns of the twenty-five-year-long war that finally destroyed the military power of the faltering Spanish monarchy. This was for the most part a very conventional war, the object not destruction of the enemy's forces but the occupation of his territory and the denial to him of yours, until eventually he was forced to resign and make peace before you

OPPOSITE An English musketeer, with his match lock, bandoliers and rest, 1640.

43

cried 'Check-mate'. It was a war of manœuvre and a war of destruction of the countryside. James thought it 'an extraordinary sight to see about ten thousand foragers, most of them with scythes in their hands, with the officers before them marching'. He does not record what the peasants thought. But above all else it was a war of siege. The whole of Picardy and French and Spanish Flanders was covered with a network of fortresses and here it was that the war was fought. Sometimes manœuvres on siege could be very complicated, as a concentric pattern of opponents built up. In the middle was the fortress with its beleaguered garrison surrounded by the investing army, whose parallel trenches zig-zagged their way towards the counterscarp. Protecting the besiegers against the danger of the arrival of a relieving army were their own carefully erected lines of circumvallation, a circle of fortifications out of reach of the garrison's guns. Beyond these might well be a relieving army, themselves opening trenches towards the besiegers, and way out in the surrounding countryside might be the besiegers' friends harassing the outliers of the relieving army. The arts of siege and relief were well-learned by the very professional French officers, who despised amateurs and scorned to rely on engineers, 'most of the officers understanding very well how to carry on a trench'.

James, a professional himself, learned all this as he rose to the rank of Lieutenant-General in the French army. No doubt he would have won a Marshal's baton if he had stayed longer. But the world of diplomacy and intrigue, to which James was forced to revert during the long periods of winter idleness in Paris, willed it otherwise. In October 1655, Cromwell, after a period of flirting with the Spaniards, made a treaty with Mazarin. An English expeditionary force, composed of the seasoned and renowned Ironsides, would fight for France in return for a large subsidy and the cession of the coveted fortress of Dunkirk, at the time held by the Spaniards. But Charles and James and seventeen other named Cavaliers were not to reside in France. James was faced with a most unpleasant choice. Was he to resign his French commission, desert his friends and fight for Spain? He was loath to do this, despite the opportunity of fighting against the soldiers of the regicides. Mazarin had no wish to lose him; he was a good soldier and,

44

more important, had attracted all the foot-loose Cavalier and Irish soldiers in Europe to the French colours. Where James went they were likely to follow. Mazarin's answer was to offer James an important post on the Italian front, an offer to which Cromwell had no objection. But Charles, intriguing now with Spain, chose otherwise and James, loyal and obedient, left to sell his sword to Spain.

James, like most other observers of the time, had a very low opinion of the Spanish generals. Don John, the son of the King of Spain by an actress, had few of the qualities of his illustrious bastard namesake who had won the Battle of Lepanto some eighty years before. His habit on arrival at a new camp was to go straight to his tent and generally to bed. Here he often stayed for days, leaving all work to his under-officers. The Marquis of Caracena was little better; another man with a passion for the siesta. What made things even worse was that all decisions had to be made by the generals, but to wake them was to court death. James's new companion-in-arms, the Prince de Condé, assured him 'that when he had served with the Spaniards as long as he had, he would get accustomed to seeing them commit grave faults without being astonished'.

The main event of this second stage of James's military career was the famous Battle of the Dunes, a battle fought and won by Turenne to prevent the Spanish relief of the siege of Dunkirk. Against the advice of Condé and nearly everyone else, the Spanish allowed themselves to be attacked in the sand-dunes outside Dunkirk. It was on this occasion that Condé made his much-quoted remark to James's younger brother, Henry, Duke of Gloucester, who at eighteen had joined him in arms: 'Were you ever in a battle?' 'No, Monsieur.' 'Well in half an hour you will see us lose one.' And so it turned out. James and Henry earned a reputation for bravery on the day which was well-deserved. Twice they charged the English Ironsides on the French left, and it was only the quality of James's armour that saved his life as good men fell around him. But the English were indestructible, and it was with much satisfaction that James described the contest, for above all he was proud of being an Englishman. 'When he had broken into this Battalion, and were got amongst them, not so much as one single man of them asked quarter, or threw down his arms; but every one defended

'Were you ever in battle? . . . in half an hour you will see us lose one'

45

himself to the last.' James was not alone in his admiration of the Redcoats, whose habit of rejoicing with cheers when they saw the enemy astonished the phlegmatic Turenne.

The defeat at the Dunes was really the end of James's military career. It was to be thirty-two years before he fought in another land battle, only, alas, to lose once again. The eighteen months following the battle were dominated for the Cavaliers in exile by the news of Cromwell's death. The intriguers thrived once again. The high-spot for James was the offer by the great Turenne himself of his own regiment of foot, arms, ammunition, ships and money, for James to invade southern England in support of Booth's rebellion in Cheshire. James emphasised that the general's offer was not on Mazarin's orders, but 'freely of himself, out of no other motive than kindness'. But Booth's rebellion was crushed before James could set sail, and at the beginning of 1660 he, like the other Cavaliers, had grown despondent, 'the hopes concerning England being now reduced to the lowest ebb'. At this time he was offered and accepted with alacrity a job which gives some indication of the reputation he had acquired in eight years' soldiering on the Continent: nothing less than command of the forces of Spain against rebellious Portugal, with the rank of High Admiral, one-fifth of all prizes and a great salary. Never before had such a post been given to any but the King's sons or near relatives – not bad for a penniless exile, even if he was a duke.

While James exulted, the most taciturn man of his age, the tobacco-chewing General Monck, had already had his call from God to march into England 'for the liberty and being of parliaments ... and a godly ministry'. Monck, a former Royalist officer who had changed sides after being captured by the Parliamentary army, was the military governor of Scotland. As he marched south with the army of Scotland, all those who desired a speedy end to the chaotic military rule that had followed the death of Cromwell, saw that only a soldier could tame the other soldiers, call a free Parliament and restore the monarchy. Monck, calculating public opinion to a nicety, saw that what was good for England was good for him, and eventually entered into negotiations with Charles. After all the plots and intrigues of the exiles, they were to have little to do with the process that restored the Stuart kings to a delighted

George Monck, the
military governor of
Scotland in 1660, who led
the negotiations for
Charles's restoration to the
throne. Miniature by
Samuel Cooper.

nation. Hyde's policy of waiting patiently till the rebels fell out
among themselves and a right-wing group invited the King to
return to rule them proved the right one. For James it must
have seemed a miracle. On 14 May 1660 he was received as
Lord High Admiral by the English fleet, only a few months
after being appointed High Admiral of Spain. James was
nervous, maybe it was all a dream. Admiral Montagu's
secretary, the eagerly climbing Mr Pepys, reported the Duke
of York sending every day to see whether he could board the
ships. At last on the 22nd, the weather calmer, he went aboard
the *London* and three days later stepped ashore on English soil.
The Duke of York had returned to his heritage, the second man
in the kingdom, twenty-six years old – a rather different
proposition to the boy in girl's clothing who had left twelve
years before. The Restoration gossip Grammont, although
often unreliable, gives us a character of James at this time which
seems to fit exactly what we know of him from other sources.
'He had a reputation for undaunted courage, meticulously
keeping his word, great economy in his affairs, hauteur,
application and arrogance in that order. Scrupulous in the rules
of duty and the laws of justice, he was regarded as a faithful
friend and an implacable enemy.' How would this character
adapt to the gay world of the Restoration?

3 Lord High Admiral

1660-8

F
EW PERIODS and places can be so well-known to the general
reader as Restoration London. Recorded forever in the
diaries of Evelyn and Pepys, in the cynical barbs of the Restoration wits and gossips, is that time when a whole city threw off
its Puritan seriousness under the eye of a wily, merry monarch.
The theatres re-opened, and *demi-mondaine* actresses in lewd
plays were the toast of the town; the churches once again
offered the beauty and grace of the Anglican service; taverns
served the enormous quantities of wine and beer that made
Mr Pepys and his friends so befuddled; Evelyn and the Royal
Society engaged in their endless pursuit of strange information
about such matters as the nature of spiders in Ireland or Mr
Boyle's *Vacuum*; above all there were the endless *amours* of a
Court in which, according to Winston Churchill, 'there was
undoubtedly an easy commerce of the sexes, marked at times
by actual immorality' – surely a masterpiece of historical under-
statement.

James commenced his life in this brave new world by a
colossal *faux-pas*. Way back in 1656, his sister Mary had brought
to her mother's Court at St Germain a big-bosomed, blue-eyed
lady-in-waiting called Anne Hyde, the daughter of the
Chancellor. She had not made much impression among the
beauties of Paris, but back in The Hague, where James was to
meet her again, she seemed a very desirable property and he, no
doubt encouraged by the strong-willed and ambitious Anne,
had wooed her. The outcome had been the signature of James
Stuart to a promise of marriage so strictly drawn up that any
child of the union would have been legitimate under English
law. A few months before the Restoration Anne had become
pregnant. 'God grant that it may be by him', wrote James's
mother to her sister the Duchess of Savoy, 'a girl who will
abandon herself to a prince will abandon herself to another.'

James in England found himself in a position of acute
embarrassment. When he had signed the contract in November
1659 he had been a soldier of fortune with few prospects. Now
he was the Duke of York, a match for any royal heiress in
Europe. Could he honour his agreement with a commoner,
the daughter of his brother's lawyer Chancellor? No, said his
mother and sister, as they hastened to England to stop the
match. No, said the Earl of Sandwich to Mr Pepys, in the crudest

PREVIOUS PAGES British
ships in the Mediterranean
in 1675.

OPPOSITE Sir Thomas
Killigrew, dramatist and
courtier. He became page
of honour to Charles I
in 1633, and remained
faithfully attached to
him, so that the King's
portrait is shown hanging
upon the wall. Killigrew's
plays are portrayed stacked
up on the table before him.
In 1663 he founded the
Theatre Royal at Drury
Lane. This portrait was
painted by W. Sheppard
while Killigrew was
Charles II's Resident in
Venice in 1650.

Restoration London

With the return of Charles II, his family and Court in 1660, London took on a new lease of life and threw off its Puritan seriousness. The Great Fire of 1666 destroyed many of the old, overcrowded sections of the City, enabling Wren and his colleagues to produce a fine new City for the Restoration monarch.

RIGHT Wenceslaus Hollar's engraving of the Royal Exchange in 1674. The Exchange was built by Sir Thomas Gresham during the reign of Elizabeth I, and by the 1660s it had become the financial nerve-centre of London and the nation.

RIGHT Lambeth Palace, with a view of Westminster across the Thames. On the left stands Whitehall Palace and in the centre, the great houses along the Strand. Painting by an imitator of Knyff. 1682.

PIAZZA in Coventgarden.

ABOVE The Piazza at Covent Garden in the 1670s. The site had been developed in the 1620s to the designs of Inigo Jones. He built the fortress-like portico of St Paul's Church, and around the flanking sides of the square, two-storeyed houses above shopping arcades.

55

possible language. No, said James's friends among the young bloods who used a time-honoured masculine device for getting out of such awkward situations, informing James that Anne was a whore and that they had all slept with her before. But Anne Hyde was no whore, and far too much in command of the situation to make such a mistake, a fact of which James was certainly aware. His instinctive belief in her fidelity must have been reinforced by the droll Thomas Killigrew, witty manager of the Theatre Royal, getting carried away in his

56

enthusiastic confession 'that the great moment had come in a certain apartment built over the water, for a purpose very different from that of giving ease to the pains of love, and that three or four swans had been witnesses to his happiness'. Even Hyde himself, now Earl of Clarendon, appeared to oppose the match, though he could hardly be displeased to see his own daughter the second lady in England. James's indecision was resolved for him by his brother, furious at his foolishness, who ordered him to marry the girl and honour his contract. Much relieved, James celebrated the marriage in secret on 3 September, and on 22 October the child, Charles, Duke of Cambridge, was born. He died as a baby of smallpox, a scourge that swept through the royal family that winter, killing James's brother Henry and his sister Mary as well as his baby son.

Despite the unfortunate circumstances of its celebration and his constant infidelity, James's marriage to Anne Hyde was a happy one, and her powerful, intelligent nature had a strong effect on his character. Both she and James were great naggers. He nagged Charles and she nagged James, but she had much more effect on James than he ever had on his brother. James's alliance with Anne Hyde tied him closely to the unpopular Lord Chancellor, his father-in-law, and to Anne's brothers who rose with their sister to take their place among the great of the land. Socially, Anne adapted with remarkable ease to the role of Duchess of York. Under the tutelage of the Queen Mother, anxious to make the best of a bad job, the 'buttered bun' of Andrew Marvell's poem became a duchess born.

James, his conscience now quiet, prepared to enjoy the Restoration scene. His amusements seem to have been confined entirely to women and hunting. He took his place in the fashionable throng at theatres and balls, but showed no interest in the literary and scientific achievements of the age, nor indeed, apart from women, in the vices of the Court. James neither drank nor gambled; his favourite beverage seems to have been a cup of tea. Hunting was his favourite pastime. Throughout his life the hard riding learned as a cavalry officer in France was to spell the doom of miserable hares and stags. James was always in at the kill, out-riding all his fellows. He is also credited with being the first to introduce fox-hunting as an aristocratic pastime, and there is something about James, charging across

57

Arabella Churchill, maid-in-waiting to Anne Hyde. She became James's mistress some time during the 1660s and retained this exalted position until 1678. Her brother was John Churchill, later Duke of Marlborough, and her eldest son by James was another celebrated soldier, the Duke of Berwick.

the English countryside with his pack of hounds in pursuit of the uneatable, that is typical of the man. As for women, James celebrated his marriage with a perfect orgy of incontinence. His reputation in this field was as bad as, if not worse than, that of his brother. He was 'the most unguarded ogler of his time'. The reader may be spared the details, but Grammont's account of James's courtship of the glamorous Miss Hamilton must be quoted. James, just back from hunting and very tired, entertained the lady with what was in his head, 'telling her miracles of the cunning of foxes and the mettle of horses; giving her accounts of broken legs and arms, dislocated shoulders and other curious and diverting adventures' until they both fell asleep. How typical of the lecherous sportsman.

But James, like another hunting womaniser, Louis XIV's son the Grand Dauphin, had a predilection for women whom his fellows considered ugly. After courting nearly all the Restoration beauties from Lady Castlemaine to Lady Chesterfield, and annoying his brother by competing in the race for La Belle Stuart's virginity, he fell madly in love with 'a tall creature, pale-faced and nothing but skin and bone, named Churchill'. Arabella Churchill, lady-in-waiting to his wife, was the daughter of a Royalist cavalry officer in straitened circumstances,

FAR LEFT Lady Chesterfield, one of the Restoration beauties to whom James paid court. Portrait by Peter Lely.

59

Sir William Coventry, secretary to James as Lord High Admiral. He was an able and dedicated member of the Navy Board, and did much to build up the strength of the Navy in the 1660s. Portrait by Riley.

and James characteristically fell in love with her on the hunting field. Arabella, a poor horsewoman, fell from her horse, and those who rushed to the rescue, the Duke among them, were amazed to find from the disorder of her dress 'that limbs of such exquisite beauty could belong to a face like Miss Churchill's'. Arabella became James's mistress some time in the mid-1660s, a position she was to retain until 1678. Among the results of James's infatuation are two whose coincidence have a certain historical elegance. Her brother John became a page in James's household, the first step in the career which was to make him England's greatest soldier as the Duke of Marlborough; and her eldest son by James, the Duke of Berwick, was to become a Marshal of France, the most distinguished general in the French army during Marlborough's wars. Such is the power of a Royalist cavalry officer's genes.

In the intervals between pursuing foxes and women James could be a serious man, very serious by the standards of the

Restoration Court. As brother to the King he had a prominent part to play in the Councils of State. As a peer he came more and more to be a regular attender at the House of Lords under the tutelage of his father-in-law, Clarendon. As Lord High Admiral, he was to play a by no means passive part in that reorganisation of the navy which is the glory of the career of the humble Samuel Pepys. In this work he was very fortunate to have the services of one of the most remarkable men of his day, his secretary, Sir William Coventry. Both Coventry and Pepys represented a new and very important type of civil servant who, in the course of the next half-century, were to revolutionise the administration of government. Experts in their job, hard-working and by the standards of the day extremely dedicated, they fulfilled a vital service, not only in seeing that the work of the various government offices was done efficiently and promptly, but also in providing a link between the Court and the mercantile community. Where previously such jobs had been filled by ignorant and idle courtiers or by merchants who put their own interests before those of the nation, men like Coventry, while by no means averse to a certain amount of personal enrichment, provided a standard of honest public service hitherto unknown. James, who otherwise has a bad record in the business of choosing his own servants, can only be commended for the good sense he showed in encouraging the careers of Coventry and Pepys. If only he had taken their advice more often and retained their services for longer, many of his troubles could have been avoided.

As it was, the men responsible for the administration of the navy, James at their head, were faced with an impossible task. Restoration England inherited from the Commonwealth the largest navy that England had ever known, a navy, moreover, which had a very considerable fighting reputation abroad. This was very different from the motley collection of royal ships and armed merchantmen which had so discomfitted the Spanish Armada. Now the navy was almost entirely composed of ships built specifically for fighting – two and three-decked ships of the line carrying up to one hundred guns and a thousand fighting men. But in 1660 this formidable weapon, the main guarantee of England's security, was in disarray. In the chaotic last years of the Interregnum there had been no money for the

61

The World of Samuel Pepys

Pepys was a man of wide interests: he was not
only a lively and humorous diarist, providing
us with one of the most vivid accounts of
Restoration London, but also a book-collector,
scientist, and naval administrator of great ability.
In 1660, he accompanied the fleet welcoming
Charles back to England, and in the same year was
appointed Clerk of the Acts of the Navy. In this
post he served under James, Duke of York, the
Lord High Admiral, and gained his full
confidence. This connection brought him serious
problems in the 1670s, for, during the scares of the
Popish Plot, he was accused of Papist leanings and
of betraying naval secrets. His career revived in
the 1680s, especially after James's accession to the
throne, but the Revolution of 1688 resulted in his
dismissal and retirement. His last years were spent
in putting in order his valuable book collection
and arranging for the creation of the Pepys
Library at Magdalene College, Cambridge.

ABOVE RIGHT Samuel
Pepys in 1666; portrait by
John Hayls.
RIGHT Naval flags which
were standardised by
Pepys while he was
working at the Navy
Office.

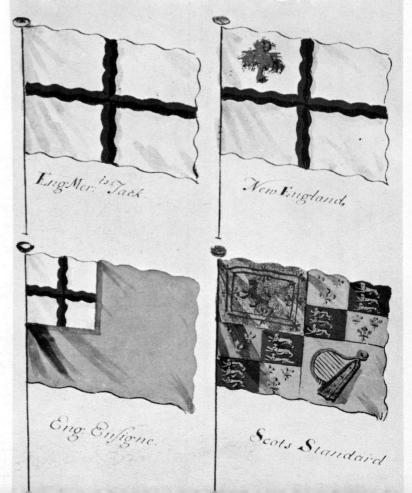

Eng. Mer.ts Jack.

New England,

Eng. Ensigne.

Scots Standard

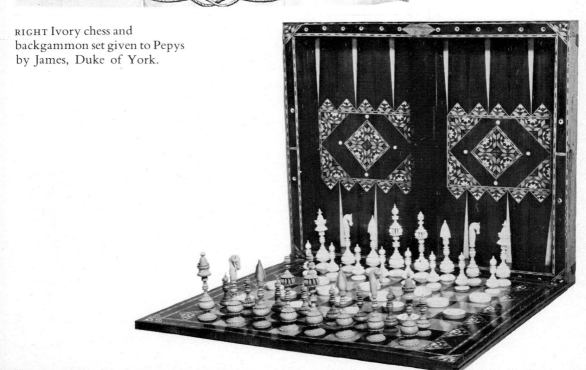

May. 31. 2669.

Mens cujusque is est quisque

LEFT The last page
of Pepys' Diary written
on 31 May 1669, when the
increasing weakness of his
eyes compelled him to
give up the project. He
wrote the diary in Thomas
Shelton's system of
tachygraphy – published
in 1641 – which he further
complicated by using
foreign language in
passages of a controversial
nature.

RIGHT Ivory chess and
backgammon set given to Pepys
by James, Duke of York.

navy, and the ships were for the most part in a very bad state of repair, while the crews were unpaid, some for as long as four years. The first task of James's Navy Board was to try to correct this appalling inheritance. Men must be paid, good ships repaired and bad ships written off, the terrible waste and corruption of the naval dockyards corrected before the English navy could justify in reality the reputation it had in Europe. But despite all the efforts of James and his subordinates the task was hopeless. For Charles, like his immediate predecessors, had not sufficient money. Clarendon, with Monck the main architect of the Restoration, had no desire to see his royal master rule without Parliament, and had therefore made sure that the funds voted to him were always just too little for him to rule alone. And the calls on these funds in the early 1660s were enormous. What Cavalier could not recite a tale of woe sufficient to soften the hardest monarch's heart? What pretty lady of the Court could not tap the royal benevolence for a new house, or at least a new wardrobe? How could a King, forced to live in penury for so long, disregard the desire of his Court for ever more magnificent masques and balls? Parliament's meanness and Charles's extravagance made the tasks of the best public servants in the country, the hard-working members of the Navy Board, impossible to perform. Although James, as Lord High Admiral and as a keen if somewhat irregular master of the navy, was aware of this, his ambitious fighting nature was stirred by the character of his job. For the Lord High Admiral was not merely an administrative officer, he also had first refusal of the command of the fleet. For a man who had spent eight years fighting in the armies of France and Spain, the possibility of leading his own country's senior service to a great victory was intoxicating. James was determined on a naval war and in this ambition he found no shortage of supporters.

England in 1660 was on the eve of that extraordinary expansion of trade and empire which was to lay the foundations of her commercial and industrial greatness in the eighteenth and nineteenth centuries. Already English ships and English merchants were trading in every quarter of the globe. The profits realised from such enterprises were making the fortunes of the merchants and financiers of the City of London. There seemed only one obstacle to a continued expansion to hitherto

LEFT Prince Rupert of the Rhine, James's first cousin, portrayed as Governor of the Hudson's Bay Company: painting by Peter Lely.
BELOW Edward Hyde, Lord Chancellor of England and James's father-in-law; portrait by Peter Lely.

undreamed of accumulation of wealth. Everywhere that English merchants sent their ships, Dutchmen were already in possession, and unfortunately those Dutchmen were much better at their job than their English rivals. Dutch ships were bigger, cheaper to build and more efficiently employed than those of England. Dutch merchants borrowed money at lower rates of interest and used it to better purpose. One answer was for Englishmen to study the methods of their rivals in Amsterdam, to copy them with no false pride, and then, by using the natural advantages of rich and fertile England, to oust the Dutchmen

Ship-building in 1675.

from the trade of the world. But, as so often happens in such a competition, any improvements made by the apprentice Englishmen were more than matched by ever greater efficiency, ever more delicate exploitation by the intelligent Dutchmen of their position as the world's *entrepôt*. The first half of the seventeenth century had seen the English falling behind in the race for the trade of the world. But there were answers to such failures in the realm of free competition. Legislation, the famous Navigation Acts, could, if properly enforced, cut the Dutch off from one of their most profitable occupations – the carrying trade between England, her Continental customers and her growing colonial empire. An even quicker answer, and one dear to James's and many others' hearts, was simply to destroy the Dutch navy and thus prevent Dutchmen from carrying on any trade at all. From the dictated peace, England would emerge unchallenged as the world's trader.

Those who supported the idea of a naval war against the United Provinces had much to encourage them. In any such war the Divine Creator, surely an Englishman, had seen fit to put geography on England's side: England's southern and eastern shores formed a crescent studded with good ports theatening the coastline of the Netherlands and every one of her trade routes, except that to the Baltic; and the prevailing wind, so vital in the days of sail, blew from England to Amsterdam giving the English an enormous tactical advantage in naval warfare. Furthermore, the Dutch economy was almost entirely dependent on trade, and any interruption to that trade would cause economic disaster within weeks. Without trade there would be insufficient food to feed the great trading cities, and insufficient raw materials to supply the great textile-processing and shipbuilding industries which were the livelihood of such a large proportion of the Dutch people. England had no such problem. Self-sufficient in food, and nearly so in raw materials, she could survive for years without suffering the catastrophe which the Dutch would experience in a few months. To such geographical and economic advantages the supporters of a war policy in England could add one more argument which, by its appeal to national pride, was all-convincing. England had already fought a naval war against the Dutch in the early 1650s and, despite some reverses, there

was no doubt that she had won it. Old sailors could still remember the glory and the prize-money, merchants the commercial gains of the First Dutch War. The pressure to fight a second one was almost irresistible.

James stood at the head of this war party. Both his brother and his father-in-law, Clarendon, opposed the idea of war. But James was adamant and in the end he had his way. James represented every one of the interest groups which pushed for war. In his simple desire for martial glory he was supported by a powerful group at Court who longed to see themselves treading a quarter-deck in a naval battle. Such was his old friend and companion-in-arms Charles Berkeley, soon to be Earl of Falmouth. As Lord High Admiral, he was supported by the professional soldiers and sailors who felt it was the main function of a navy to fight and win wars. Such were Monck, now Duke of Albemarle, Prince Rupert, Sir William Penn and the Earl of Sandwich, all of whom had much experience of fighting both on land and at sea in an age when leadership rather than seamanship was often considered the most important attribute of an admiral. Monck had amused his subordinates in the Commonwealth navy by ordering the ships to 'Right Wheel', but for all that he had enjoyed a successful naval career. Finally, James, rather strangely, represented the clamours of the City of London for a naval war. The early 1660s were distinguished, among other things, by a burst of enthusiasm for colonial adventure, and the great merchants and financiers who sponsored these activities knew better than to forget to cut in the Court on the expected profits of their promotions. Who better to encourage Court money and Court privileges to further their aims than the nationalistic, navy-loving James, Duke of York? And so we find James, as Chairman of the Royal African Company, presiding over meetings in his rooms at Whitehall, authorising the adventurous Captain Robert Holmes to take three royal ships to West Africa to seize trading-posts from the Dutch, long before the official outbreak of war. The Company had mixed fortunes, and in 1664 Pepys noted that the English had been 'beaten to dirt at Guinny by de Ruyter and his fleet'. But the net outcome was that the English broke the Dutch monopoly of the slave trade to America, and James and the other shareholders undoubtedly

OPPOSITE Anne Hyde, daughter of the Lord Chancellor, Edward Hyde, and James's first wife. She had a strong influence over James and encouraged him in his move toward the Catholic Church and his eventual conversion. Portrait by Peter Lely.

England's First Colonial Empire

James played an important part in the extraordinary expansion of trade and empire which characterised the 1660s. He was chairman of the Royal African Company and authorised the dispatch of ships to seize Dutch trading posts in West Africa. He was a shareholder in the East India Company and supported the Company's policy of establishing factories along the Indian coast and of attacking the Dutch monopoly in the Spice Islands. And it was in James's name that an unprovoked attack was made on the Dutch possessions in North America, which resulted in the name of the major city and trading centre being changed from New Amsterdam to New York in his honour.

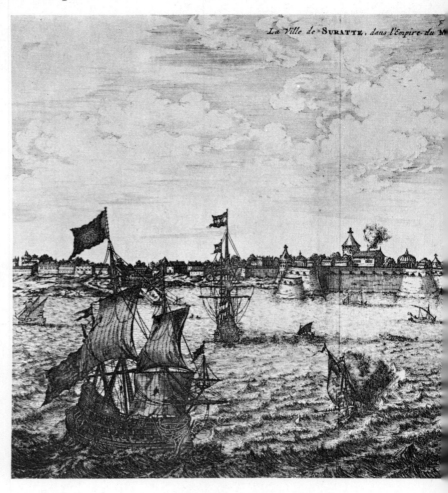

La Ville de SURATTE, dans l'Empire du M

RIGHT The lodgings and factory of the East India Company at Surat, in 1638.

The LODGINGS of the ARTISANS belonging to the COMPANY.

LEFT The city of Surat, which grew up on the site where the English first established a factory on the mainland of India. In 1612, Captain Best destroyed Portuguese naval supremacy and made Surat the seat of the presidency under the East India Company. The city began to decline after 1668, when Bombay was ceded to the Company and became the capital of the Company's possessions.

BELOW The first page of the charter of 2 May 1670, granted by Charles II to Prince Rupert and seventeen other courtiers, incorporating them as 'Governor and Company of Adventurers of England trading into Hudson's Bay'. This secured to them a monopoly of the trade of all lands watered by streams flowing into Hudson's Bay.

felt no pricks to their consciences as they pocketed the dividends earned in the carriage of this miserable human cargo. Nor was Africa the limit of James's ambitions as a merchant-prince. He was a shareholder in the East India Company and thus had an interest in the destruction of the Dutch stranglehold on the profitable trade of the Spice Islands. And on the other side of the world his interests were to result in an extraordinary memorial to his name, for in February 1664 a bill was prepared granting to the Duke of York 'lands in America from St Croix to Long Island', regardless of the fact that these lands were occupied by the Dutch. Later that year, an expedition, probably once more under the command of the ubiquitous Captain Holmes, seized these lands and out of respect for his master changed the name of the major city and trading centre from New Amsterdam to New York. The most important gap in the long chain of English possessions on the North American seaboard was plugged by this act of unprovoked aggression.

Thus, long before the official outbreak of the Second Dutch War in February 1665, the English and Dutch had been fighting each other in the far-flung corners of the world. This only served to illustrate the global nature of the contest which was about to begin. Pepys noted the opinion of one of the biggest naval contractors of his day: 'The trade of the world is too little for us two, therefore one must down.' All the various objections to the war were brushed aside. The two best-informed officials on the Navy Board, Coventry and Pepys, were both aware that the navy was not yet ready for such a contest, and Coventry knew well the sort of resistance the English were likely to experience from the desperate Dutchmen: 'The Dutch are not to be trampled on, if you do they will kick. Their trade is their God, if you depress that by any force, they will venture all for it.' But the opinions of such people did not impress the Court, or their royal master, and eventually a reluctant Charles received from an enthusiastic Parliament what seemed to be a generous supply of money for the war. It was not to be nearly enough.

At long last James's chance had come. In early May 1665, on board his eighty-gun flagship, the *Royal Charles*, he weighed anchor in command of an English fleet of over a hundred men-of-war and auxiliaries and set sail for the Dutch

coast. The initial enthusiasm of the twenty thousand men in the fleet must have been dampened by the fact that the beer ran out after only one day. James indeed had been in far too much of a hurry. There was not enough beer, not enough food, not enough of anything. And while he bravely took up the position vacated by Blake at the end of the First Dutch War, blockading the Dutch ports, the Dutch fleet remained in harbour, eager though they were to smash their rivals. For James had been too quick not only for his own suppliers, but also for those of the enemy. It must have been a frustrated James who turned back to England after only ten days at sea to pick up more stores. With his ships revictualled and deficiencies in men made up by pressing experienced sailors from a fleet of Newcastle colliers, James again set sail on 30 May to seek the Dutch, now reported to be at sea. Once more the sailors' ladies were kicked out of the hammocks from which a contemporary naval chaplain had wondered to see their 'legs to the hams hanging over the sides or out at the end'. Once more the trumpets sounded 'Loth to depart' and 'Maids where are your hearts'. As the weeping ladies waved to their departing husbands and lovers, the English and Dutch fleets sailed to battle, for the

The Battle of Lowestoft, which took place on 3 June 1665 between the English fleet under James, and the Dutch fleet commanded by Opdam. Drawing by Willem van de Velde.

73

admirals on both sides had decided on the same policy, to seek out the enemy battle-fleet and destroy it.

The two fleets were very evenly matched in ships and men, though it is probable that the English had an advantage in their guns, which on the whole were bigger and more accurate. The English, too, were the main innovators in the advance of naval tactics during this period. They were the first to see naval warfare as primarily an artillery duel instead of a rather clumsy floating land battle. They were the first to develop the line-ahead formation, the logical formation for a fighting weapon whose strength lay in the broadside cannon on its two or three decks, rather than in the massive ram which stood at the bow of the now anachronistic galley. The Dutch had followed the English, but still clung to a certain extent to the view that naval warfare was about boarding and hand-to-hand fighting, rather than the destruction of enemy ships with guns. If the Dutch had somewhat archaic ideas about tactics, they almost certainly had the better seamen, and furthermore had a reputation throughout the world for desperate courage. Rather than surrender his ship, it was said, a Dutchman would set fire to the powder magazine, blowing himself, his ship and maybe his enemy to kingdom come. Moreover, and this was to be vital in the war ahead, the Dutch had a readier supply of money with which to equip their fleet.

Early on the morning of 3 June the two fleets were in sight of each other, some fourteen miles from Lowestoft. The English had already won the vital first stage of a naval battle in the days of sail – the weather-gauge. Their whole fleet lay between the Dutch and the south-west wind which filled their sails as they bore down on the enemy. This gave them a tremendous advantage in manoeuvrability and also kept them relatively clear of smoke when the battle started. The battle itself was played in three parts, the first two a formal long-range artillery duel and the third a bloody mêlée in which ship battered ship at close range. There was a certain beauty and an extraordinary compliancy on the part of the Dutch as they followed the English lead during the formal part of the battle. The English, in a long line ahead, sailed north and the Dutch sailed south. As the ships passed each other, a manoeuvre which took several hours, they plied each other with their guns. Little damage was done. Then both fleets tacked and passed each other again, the English now sailing south and the Dutch north. But, at the third turn, James, and no doubt most courageous spirits, had had enough of this elegant ballet. Announcing that he wished to have a bout with Opdam, the Dutch admiral, whose flagship like his was in the centre of the line, he ordered the whole fleet to go about again and run parallel with the Dutch to seek out their opposite number and destroy him.

The battle now broke up into a number of ship-to-ship encounters. Damaged ships withdrew from the battle to refit and sometimes a single ship found herself surrounded by several of the enemy. In the centre, James, standing apparently nerveless on the quarter-deck, had a tremendous close-range artillery duel with Opdam. It was here that he was to suffer a great personal tragedy. Standing at his side, his great friend Charles Berkeley, Earl of Falmouth, was smashed to pieces by a Dutch chain-shot. James was more affected by Berkeley's death than by any other in his whole life. Public opinion did not quite share his high opinion of his friend and was probably expressed in the wicked lines of the poet Sir John Denham, who wrote of Berkeley's death:

> His shattered head the fearless Duke distains,
> And gave the last first proof that he had brains.

'*And gave the last first proof that he had brains*'

Soon after Berkeley's death a lucky shot struck Opdam's magazine and the Dutch flagship blew up. It was the signal for the rest of the Dutch fleet, who had been having much the worst of the close-range combat, to turn and run for home.

It was then that James was to be the victim of one of those colossal pieces of bad luck which dogged his career and exaggerated disasters which could be attributed to the obvious defects of his character. He had just won in open combat the most conclusive victory of all the Dutch wars. To make his victory permanent, and put his name among such men as Drake and Blake in the annals of victorious sailors, he had only to pursue and destroy the battered Dutch, who up to this point had only lost about a quarter of their battle fleet. James gave the order to crowd on sail and pursue, and then at about eleven o'clock, after some eighteen hours on deck, went below to get some sleep. While James slept, all his success was belittled by the extraordinary action of an officer of his household, Henry Brounker, who managed to persuade the officer of the watch to shorten sail, an action followed by the rest of the English fleet. Whether he was acting on the orders of James's wife to save her royal husband from any further risk, or whether he was himself a coward who had seen enough of naval action for a lifetime, we shall never know. What is certain is that when James awoke, the Dutch were clean away and the best chance of a really decisive victory in the whole war had gone.

The Battle of Lowestoft still made James a naval hero, and the story of his courage was to be remembered in later years when the character of the Duke of York was to come in for almost universal condemnation. But James himself was given no chance to repeat his victory. Alarmed at the possibility that his brother, and the only obvious adult heir to the throne, might share the fate of Berkeley, Charles forbade James to go to sea again. For the rest of the war, James was a frustrated observer from the land of the miserable, and ultimately disastrous, English fortunes. Even before the Battle of Lowestoft, the Great Plague had broken out in London and it was to be followed in the succeeding year by the Great Fire. It was, therefore, a very wretched London that heard of the repeated disasters of the Second Dutch War. As Coventry had prophesied, the Dutch were not to be trampled on, and their kicks hurt. As the news poured in, it was obvious that the English, the aggressive initiators of the war, were losing. Not even the fantastic courage of Monck against odds in the Four Days' Battle, nor the successful commerce-raiding of Captain Holmes, could disguise that. The main reason for England's failure was equally obvious – lack of supply. Neither Parliament nor the City had counted on a long war, and neither was prepared to subsidise a losing cause; least of all the City, whose losses in the Great Fire had been enormous. With no money, the task of Pepys, Coventry and their fellows at the Navy Board was hopeless. They knew the sailors were starving or deserting to the Dutch, whose dollars seemed infinitely more attractive than the miserable tickets – promises to pay which could only be cashed at enormous discounts – handed out by the bankrupt English naval authorities. They knew why the dockyard workers refused to work and the rotten ships were foundering.

76

So did James; and one can sympathise with his annoyance at Pepys's constant demands for money. For James had no more power to produce cash than anyone else. His erstwhile colleagues in the East India Company had long given up the war as a bad job and only hoped the peace would not be too bad. In the end, James was forced, very reluctantly, to take an appalling step for a Lord High Admiral. In order to save money, the great ships of the English navy were laid up in the middle of a naval war, and all the available cash was to be used for financing commerce-raiders and strengthening the coastal defences against the expected Dutch invasion. Now the Dutch were really masters of the seas. With complete impunity they were able to blockade the mouth of the Thames. Worse was to follow. In the middle of June 1667 the Dutch sailed up the Medway, broke through the chain which guarded the river and, virtually unresisted, towed away James's old flagship, the *Royal Charles*,

The burning of the English fleet on the Medway by the Dutch Admiral, de Ruyter, in June 1667: painting by William Schellinks.

and fired a number of other men-of-war. A terrified London waited to see what they would do next. 'By God', said one of Pepys's colleagues, 'I think the Devil shits Dutchmen.'

It was fortunate for England that the Dutch wanted peace almost as much as did the English. What the Dutch did in the Medway was dramatic and humiliating, but it is a sign of Dutch weakness that they did no more. They would have had little opposition if they had sent a force up-river to burn down what was left of London. But the Dutch, too, were exhausted by the most expensive naval war ever known, and all Dutch instincts were directed towards making peace and resuming the normal pattern of trade. The Dutch attitude had been summed up by the Grand Pensionary, John de Witt, before the outbreak of war: 'If the Devil himself were sovereign of England it would be necessary to live on friendly terms with him.' For this reason, and also from fear of their ally, France, the Dutch made peace

at Breda in 1667 on very reasonable terms. There was to be some relaxation of the Navigation Laws in the favour of the victorious Hollanders, but New York was to remain English, as were one or two strongholds in West Africa. Overall it was a very kind peace to the humiliated English.

For James, the disasters of England were personal disasters. As Lord High Admiral, fairly or unfairly, he was forced to take much of the blame for the irresponsible way in which the war had been run. The hero of Lowestoft was forgotten in the days of plague, fire and naval disaster. As brother to the King and a dissolute member of a dissolute and corrupt Court, he received his share of the hatred felt by starving and homeless Londoners for the ostentation and apparent indifference of the wealthy courtiers, whose great homes being built in the fashionable West End mocked their fellows sheltering in temporary shacks or cellars under the blackened ruins of the City. The fact that both James and Charles had tried to do their best to stem the passage of the fire was also forgotten. The story remembered by Pepys, one of the few men who made money out of the war, was that the King and Lady Castlemaine had chased a moth about the royal mistress's supper room, while the Dutch burned the royal fleet in the Medway.

James suffered also from his loyal support of his father-in-law. For the whole of the 1660s a clique of courtiers, led by Bennet and the Duke of Buckingham, had been trying to get rid of Charles's elderly counsellor, whose moral uprightness and disapproval they found so annoying. In 1667 they were successful, and Clarendon became the scapegoat for an unsuccessful war which he had opposed and Bennet and Buckingham had supported. Almost the only man to speak up for him was James, a fact which annoyed Charles and led to a serious breach between the brothers. In 1668, James, who had been so much sought after by merchants and courtiers at the Restoration and had been a national hero in the first year of the war, found himself without any support whatsoever. Even Coventry had gone, defeated by the same combination of Bennet and Buckingham which had destroyed Clarendon. Sir William Coventry being gone, the Duke of York will have no 'sure friend to stick to him', wrote Pepys, 'nor any good man will remain to advise what is good'. Pepys's judgment was only too accurate.

4 The Convert 1668-73

I T IS SURELY SIGNIFICANT that at this low point in James's career he should make the most important decision of his life. For it was in 1668, deserted for the moment by most of his former colleagues and friends, that he asked to be admitted to the Roman Communion. There is considerable mystery about the circumstances of his conversion. What is certain is that it was a gradual process; James had no flash of insight into the mysteries of salvation on some road to Damascus. As we have seen, he was brought up a strict member of the Anglican Church. He seems to have had no religious doubts before his flight to the Continent in 1648, and there is no evidence whatsoever that his mother was responsible for his conversion. Indeed, from what we know of James's relations with his mother, it would seem more likely that any religious approaches from Henrietta Maria would have strengthened his Anglicanism rather than suborned it. Certainly in 1654, James had joined Charles in a very strong protest against his mother's attempt to convert his young brother Henry.

Nevertheless it was in France that James first began to have doubts. A nun in Flanders was said to have pressed James about his religion, and her entreaty to him to pray to God every day 'that if he was not in the right way He would bring him to it' made a deep impression on him. Furthermore, the fact that Catholics were not the immoral reprobates they were made out to be by Protestant Englishmen was obvious in the most casual observation of his brother-officers in the French army, and James was much impressed by the exemplary lives of many French Catholics, and particularly of converts. The view that Catholics were entitled to respect was one shared by many Anglican Cavaliers who had lived abroad, and gave them a desire for general toleration not shared by the majority of their stay-at-home countrymen. In the early 1660s, the Court generally, and James in particular, were criticised for their friendliness to Catholics and their willingness to employ them in their households, and Charles's attempt to honour his pledge to provide a 'liberty to tender consciences' made in his Declaration of Breda died a rapid death at the hands of the Anglican reaction represented in the Cavalier Parliament.

But toleration is a long way from conversion, and there is no reason to believe that James was anything more than sym-

PREVIOUS PAGES Satire of 1680, showing the terrible prospects of a Popish successor to the English throne.

84

Diamond point etching
on glass of the portrait
of James as Duke of
York. English work of
about 1660.

pathetic to the Old Religion in 1660. His interest in the subject
was, however, sufficient to lead him to try to discover why the
reformed Churches had broken away. He read Hooker and the
Scriptures; he discussed the problem with Anglican divines.
The more he read and the more he thought about the subject,
the more he became convinced that Jesus Christ had left behind
him an infallible Church, and that this Church was the Church
of Rome. During the period in which he was moving towards
this monumental truth, he must have been encouraged at every
step by his domineering and intellectually much brighter wife,
Anne, for she was following almost exactly the same path. How
powerful must have been her influence in that depressing part
of James's life at the end of the Dutch War. Not only did she
encourage him and strengthen his resolve, but she also set him
the example. For it is almost certain that Anne was admitted

to the Roman Communion before James.

Once James had decided on the truth of the Roman Church, nothing on earth could shake him from his decision. And this is nothing less than one would expect from the brave and resolute man he was at this time in his life. His Catholicism was to bring him nothing but disaster in this world, but he never wavered. And indeed if he really believed in the truth of the religion, as he undoubtedly did, why should he waver? What were disappointments in this life compared with the prospects of salvation and eternal happiness in the next? In private James was to thank God that He in his wisdom had sent him into exile in France, and thus set him on that path which would lead to his conversion. Ten years after his conversion, James was to write to his friend George Legge, who had attempted to get him to renounce his religion: 'Pray once for all never say anything to me again of turning Protestant; do not expect it or flatter yourself that I shall ever be it; I never shall. What I have done was not done hastily, but upon mature consideration, and foreseeing all and more than has yet happened to me.' Once James had shown to the world that he was a Catholic, he would do nothing to lessen the embarrassment he caused to his friends and colleagues or the hatred he aroused in the minds of the majority of Protestant Englishmen. In 1669 he consulted a Jesuit on the possibility of still attending Anglican services, in spite of his acceptance into the Roman Church. He was told that there was no justification whatsoever in hiding his faith. This was a fairly extreme view in the England of his time, but James accepted it without question. A few years later, when not only his own future but that of the whole monarchy was under fire, he refused to listen to a very reasonable plea by some of the Anglican bishops that he would appear side by side with his brother in the Anglican Chapel Royal. They did not ask him to take the sacrament in the Anglican rite, or to avoid Mass, but he was adamant in his refusal. 'My principles do not allow me to dissimulate my religion after this fashion', he replied. 'I cannot resolve to do evil that good may come of it.' He was a very obstinate man.

James's conversion completely changed him. He lost any grace or gaiety he may have had as a young man. We have seen that his conversion was an intellectual rather than an emotional

'My principles do not allow me to dissimulate my religion'

86

experience, and there is in his Catholicism none of that beauty and love of show which make the Church so attractive to many. Nor is there any of that simplicity and wonder at the miracles of creation. James's Catholicism is cold, and his devotional papers are full of the conviction that once having discovered the truth he has a certainty of salvation, if only he could keep himself up to the mark. But therein lies the difficulty, for James was only too aware that morally he was a weak man. He regretted with real penitence that he had 'so very foolishly and indiscreetly exposed myself to sin'. Repeatedly he longed for death; the shorter his life the less chance of his falling. Because James found it so difficult to resist temptation himself, he assumed that this was true of all converts, and recommended his own dreary life to others. In particular he warned them to avoid the world as much as possible: 'Be cautious of theatres and balls which are very dangerous to frequent.' And if it was socially essential to go to such potentially dangerous gatherings, 'govern your eyes with discretion, remembering how many people are at the point of death at that very time'. Indeed the only place that James felt really safe was on the hunting field. His praise of such innocent recreations as hunting and shooting recalls the justifications of that great fourteenth-century hunter Gaston Phoebus, who thought that God loved hunters because they had no time to sin. For all James's mortification, he was totally unable to avoid the temptations set before him every day in the Court, and he broke the seventh commandment with monotonous regularity. 'I less than any other can say I have lived up to what I professed since I was reconciled', he confessed sadly in the solitude of his study. No wonder that Nell Gwynne, the star of Drury Lane, should call him 'dismal Jimmy'! One feels that Charles was right in his gibe that James chose ugly women to mortify himself.

Converts were only a small minority of the Catholics in England at this time, though, in their conviction and their Jesuit-inspired insistence on proselytising, they had an influence far greater than their numbers alone would have suggested. Most English Catholics were men and women who had never left the Old Religion. It was, after all, only a century since Catholics had formed the vast majority of the English population, and even in 1660 after persecution and, theoretically, an

James, the Indefatigable Huntsman

Hunting was James's favourite pastime, and he loved to outride his companions and be present at the kill. He is credited with being the first to introduce fox-hunting into England as an aristocratic pastime.

RIGHT Franz Snyders's canvas of a fox-hunt.

ABOVE Two engravings by Wenceslaus Hollar of hunting. *Left* Hawking of herons. *Right* Coursing fallow deer with greyhounds.

The blest St. Mathewes Sacred memory
Stands in this month, fix'd to posterity:
Th'Archangell Michaell, or Christ named so,
Did foyle the Dragon, our soules mortall foe.

The Sunn's in Libra, with his restless rest,
And day and night with equall howres are drest:
Now sommer shewes his back, and winters face
With time doth steale vppon the Worlds space.

St. Luke who did the Glorious Ghospell write
And th'Acts of all th'Apostles well endite:
St. Simon, and St. Iudas, all these three
In this month, by the Church remembred be.

The Countrey swaynes their harvest being don
Then vp to Westminster this Tearme they run:
And as they reapt the feilds quite bare of graine
Their follyes there doth reape them bare of gaine.

Of All Saints blest and cursed Powder plott
Must never be by Protestants forgott
St. Andrew ends as All Saints doth begin
And may we (as they did) salvation win.

The feilds and trees are all disrob'd againe,
Starke naked strip'd of flowers, of hearbes, and fruites,
And now, the Lord, the Low the Sir, the Swayne,
If they be wise (and can) will procure warme suites.

St. Thomas and our Saviour Iesus Christ.
St. Steuen and St. Iohn th'Evangelist,
And th'Inocents, their dayes this month doth hallow.
And as they lead the way, God grannt we followe.

He thats a mizer all the yeare beside
Will Revell now and for no cost will spare
A pox hang sorrow lett the world goe slide
Now every Cobler like a King will fare.

appalling body of penal legislation, they formed at least one-tenth and possibly much more of the population. In the statute book existed a vast array of laws against Catholics, carrying penalties which increased in severity the more zealously and openly a person practised his religion. Simple failure to attend Anglican services carried a fine of a shilling for every absence. Refusal to receive the Anglican sacrament was met by a fine of £20 in the first year, and steeply rising fines in succeeding years. The celebration of Mass carried higher penalties, while the death penalty could be imposed for harbouring priests or attempting to convert a non-Papist. Such fines were enormous by the standards of the day, when a skilled workman could only expect to earn some 1/6d a day, and, if the laws had ever been put fully into force, there is no doubt that the Catholic religion would have been totally extinguished many years before. The truth was, however, that a considerable measure of toleration existed in fact, if not in law. Both Charles I and Charles II were sympathetic to Catholics and did little to encourage the enforcement of the laws against Popish recusants, as offenders were called. In the years before the Civil War, for instance, the average fine per convicted recusant was only some £2 per head, and few Catholics were convicted. For all this,

ABOVE Esselen's painting of a landscape with coach, painted soon after the Restoration. This picture is remarkable in that it is one of the few accomplished landscapes painted in England at this period. The building in the distance on the right is Hampton Court Palace.

OPPOSITE A Mummer's Almanac, from the mid-seventeenth century, showing the last four months of the year.

91

Catholics remained a persecuted minority, liable at any time to a sudden tightening of the penal laws, as a result of some upsurge of popular hatred, or simply from the wish of the government to benefit from such a useful source of supplementary revenue.

Faced with such a paraphernalia of disabilities, few Catholics, even converts, were as open in the profession of their faith as James. Indeed, in the spectrum of religious beliefs in seventeenth-century England, there were many people whose inner convictions told them that the Catholic religion was the right one, but whose uncourageous common-sense told them that they would get on much better in this world if they toed the Anglican line. Such was a Church Papist, a man who:

> ... loves Popery well but is loth to lose by it. Once a month he presents himself at the [Anglican] church to keep off the churchwardens, kneels with the congregation, but prays by himself and asks God's forgiveness for coming thither. He would make a bad martyr and a good traveller, for his conscience is so large he could never wander from it, and in Constantinople would be circumcised with a mental reservation.

Together with the Papists who thus appeared to be Anglicans, we must place the Anglicans with doubts but not much strength of character. These were the people who went in for spectacular death-bed conversions, either to hedge their bets like Charles II, or to declare openly a long-felt conviction. James felt worried about the efficacy of death-bed conversion. Not only was it rather unfair to win salvation in the last minutes of one's life, after a career of unbridled sin, but it was also very risky. What happens if there are no priests around? And would God Himself play the game? 'Though God be a God of mercy and of long suffering, yet his justice is terrible, and will reward every one according to his works.'

The strength of English Catholicism rested in the large number of people who made no secret of their faith, and accepted with long-suffering good humour the limitations and ordeals forced on them by hostile public opinion. When times were good and the laws were relaxed they were happy. When the almost inevitable reaction came, they pulled in their belts and prepared to survive until the popular fury which had initiated it had subsided. Such a man was the Royalist soldier

'Though God be a God of mercy ... yet his justice is terrible'

and invincible Popish recusant William Blundell, a country gentleman from Lancashire, an area where the Old Religion was particularly strong. He had a very hard time during the Civil War and Commonwealth when, like most of his fellows, he was prosecuted both as a delinquent (Royalist) and as a recusant. Four times in prison, forced to sell lands to pay his fines, he never despaired as he struggled to bring up his large family in his faith. He risked enormous fines to educate his children in English convents and seminaries abroad. To correspond with them he had to use assumed names and often write in code. The daughters became nuns and his eldest son a Jesuit father in the English mission, an outlaw who every day ran the risk of being betrayed and tortured to death. For Blundell to entertain his son in his own house was again to risk death for harbouring a priest. Through these trials and dangers he heard Mass regularly and never faltered in his religion. From his simple statement of his philosophy it is easy to see what attracted men to the Roman Church: 'These are our known principles by the strict practising of which we shall live and die with comfort, though poor and passing to our last home by the gibbet.' There were thousands of men like William Blundell in Restoration England.

It was to be five years from his conversion before James finally and irrevocably announced his Catholicism to a hostile world. Long before then he had recovered from the position of isolation in which he found himself at the end of the Second Dutch War. For some years after the fall of Clarendon in 1667, Charles took as his advisers a heterogeneous collection of five men, whose only common opinion had been opposition to Clarendon. They were known as the Cabal from the coincidence of their initials forming that word. Thomas Clifford was a follower of Arlington. He stood on the right in all three of the spheres that were going to be so ardently discussed in the next five years. He was a Catholic, a firm believer in despotic monarchy, and his foreign policy was anti-Dutch and pro-French. Arlington, whom we have already met as Henry Bennet, was to die a Catholic and believed in following Charles's policy wherever it might lead, not an easy thing to do. He was married to a Dutch lady and was pro-Spanish, so it was difficult to guess what he would do or advise in foreign policy.

Buckingham, whom we have met as James's playmate and later companion-in-arms in France, was almost totally irresponsible. His political career, like his love affairs, was designed to amuse him, and few contemporaries would have been so unwise as to suggest that he had any policy at all. Anthony Ashley Cooper, later Earl of Shaftesbury, was far and away the most gifted of the five ministers. His career, which reads like a masterpiece of time-serving and well-calculated desertion of succeeding masters, was in fact much more logical and consistent than at first appears. The man who had served and deserted both Charles I and Cromwell believed throughout his life in what was later to be called Whiggery, and he himself has some claim to be called the first Whig. He believed in monarchy, but a monarchy totally subordinated to Parliament, and his ideal Parliament would have had an even more restricted franchise than existed, so that only extremely rich men like himself could sit in it. Parallel to his hatred of absolute monarchy was a hatred of Catholicism, which was later to be joined by a hatred and fear of the rapidly growing power of the French monarchy. For the moment, however, he belonged to those who opposed the commercial might of the Dutch Republic, and his most famous speech as Charles's minister was a passionate plea for continuation of war against the Dutch, in which he compared the Anglo-Dutch struggle to the Punic Wars. An efficient administrator, he was also a genius at leading and manipulating men, a gift which he was to use unsparingly. The last member of the Cabal was Lauderdale, the intelligent, cruel, coarse Scottish nobleman who had ruled Scotland with an iron hand since the Restoration.

Very soon after James's return to favour he found himself almost a sixth member of the Cabal, and the one who was closest to Charles's ear. Charles put up manfully with the endless nagging of his converted brother and indeed often followed his advice, at least on small things where he could submit without any serious effect. But there was a great matter in Charles's mind, and to put this into execution he must rely on his own canniness.

Charles's policy as King resolved into two major ambitions, each incompatible with the other. He would have lived

Charles II, an unfinished miniature from life by Samuel Cooper.

to have been an absolute monarch ruling a Catholic State without the impertinent aid of Parliament – the equivalent in fact of his very successful royal cousin, Louis XIV of France. On the other hand he was a lazy, pleasure-loving man who wanted above all never to go on his travels again and recoiled with horror at the threat of civil violence. Considering how totally irreconcilable two such views were in contemporary England, his was a remarkable achievement. He died the most successfully absolute of English seventeenth-century monarchs, the happy ruler of an outwardly happy State – his only failure was that the State he ruled remained uncompromisingly Protestant. It was his apparent determination to make it Catholic that dominated his policies during the period of the Cabal.

The keystone to Charles's policy was the notorious secret Treaty of Dover signed in May 1670. This is one of the most startling obligations ever imposed on a fortunately ignorant nation. By it Charles was to receive a large subsidy from Louis XIV to raise an army and re-equip the navy. In return he was to co-operate with Louis in the total destruction of the Dutch Republic and partition of its empire; and to declare

95

his Catholicism. Finally, he was to lead England back to the Church of Rome, and, in the event of civil disturbance following such an attempt, Louis pledged himself to support him with French troops. The total unreality of such a scheme has led most historians to assume that Charles signed the treaty with his tongue in his cheek, for it seems that the treaty was likely to offend almost every English prejudice. An army paid with French money would theoretically enable Charles to do without Parliament and would therefore be opposed by almost every country gentleman whom Parliament represented. The Civil War had been fought for less than this. How much worse, then, was the idea to use this army to impose Catholicism on a Protestant nation. On the third point opinion was divided. There were many who felt that the Dutch should be taught a lesson after the humiliations of the Second Dutch War. But there were others, perhaps more realistic, who felt that the French were far and away more dangerous than the Dutch. For France was no longer the divided nation it had been in James's youth. Since the death of Mazarin in 1661, Louis XIV had ruled as the most absolute of absolute monarchs. He and his subordinates had turned the French army into the most formidable fighting machine in the world. To the south and east there was little to stop the march of this colossus. The two great Habsburg powers, Spain and Austria, the obvious balance to French ambitions, had been reduced to pale shadows of their former military greatness by the Thirty Years' War and its aftermath. There seemed nothing to check the advance of French influence, but a combination of the Protestant powers of northern Europe, and this was indeed the official English policy when Charles signed the Treaty of Dover. Only two years before, he had committed himself to a Triple Alliance with Sweden and the United Provinces. But Charles and even Ashley, who was later to be the violent opponent of France, were not worried by the Continental expansion of France. They felt, like many Englishmen before and since, that England's insular position and naval strength were quite sufficient to protect her against invasion from the Continent. What seemed important was French money, French support for Charles's ambitions to rule as an absolute monarch, and the prospect of the residual gains to be made in trade and territory by the destruction of the Dutch. He

OPPOSITE Henrietta of Orléans, James's youngest sister, who was married in 1660 to Philip, Duke of Orléans, Louis XIV's unpleasant brother. She acted as Charles II's chief agent in promoting the secret Treaty of Dover.

96

failed to note what worried many of his contemporaries, the fact that Louis's great minister, Colbert, had built up the French navy and French commerce to such an extent that the French now seemed to be as great, if not greater, competitors in the struggle for the commerce of the world, in which just ten years before there had been only two contestants.

Most historians assume, probably correctly, that the secret Treaty of Dover was a massive piece of confidence trickery on the part of Charles. It is thought that the only real object of the treaty was to get a large subsidy from Louis XIV, which would enable Charles to forego the humiliating demands for money which he was repeatedly forced to make to his own Parliament. This may well be true, but if so, Charles certainly made fools of most of his ministers and of nearly all his subjects, as well as of his friends. Above all, he made a fool not only of his brother James but also of his only surviving and favourite sister, Minette, who was Louis XIV's sister-in-law and Charles's chief agent in promoting the treaty. Furthermore, by inserting the religious clauses in the treaty, he laid himself open to a constant threat of blackmail in the future, for if these clauses had ever been revealed to the public, Charles's position would have been extremely awkward. As it turned out, he never in fact received nearly enough French money, either to pay his already enormous debts or to fight the war, and he was forced to go to Parliament to get what he needed. Ironically, the answer to his money problem, and thus eventually to the possibility of ruling without Parliament, was neutrality. Between 1674 and 1678 Charles was neutral, while France and the Netherlands continued to pound away at each other. England's neutrality enabled her to carry goods for and seize trade from both the belligerents, thus swelling the customs revenue, granted for life to Charles in 1660, to unprecedented heights.

James was first let in on the secret of Charles's Grand Design in January 1669. At a secret meeting in James's rooms, Charles announced his conversion to James, the two Catholic sympathisers in the Cabal, Arlington and Clifford, and the most respected of the Catholic peers, Lord Arundel of Wardour. He asked them to advise him on the best means of making his conversion public and of settling the Catholic religion in England. It needs no imagination to realise the enthusiasm with which the newly-converted and politically unrealistic James heard this bombshell. Once converted, it was James's duty, and one he never shrank from, to save the souls of his misguided fellow-countrymen. By persuasion, example and the use of his political position, he must, if he wished to be saved himself, try with all his might to increase the possibility of salvation of others. His joy at hearing that his brother was himself committed to the same path was unbounded. For the rest of his life this Grand Design was to be his main objective. No doubt Charles was embarrassed by James's continual pressure to forward his policies at any cost, but at least he was not allowed to forget them. He was also embarrassed by the fact that he was forced to try to carry out his policy without the knowledge of three of his five chief ministers, the Protestants Buckingham, Ashley and Lauderdale. The way he did this was characteristically crafty. He allowed Buckingham to make and earn the glory of a second secret treaty with France, similar to his own, but without the religious clauses.

After some delay, Charles actually began to implement the policy established by the Treaty of Dover. On 15 March 1672 he made his Declaration of Indulgence, a royal command for religious toleration in the kingdom, an obvious first step if he was to 'settle' the Catholic religion in England. Two days later, he declared war on the Dutch, disregarding his two-year-old alliance with them. At every stage James was at his shoulder, and in fact did much to precipitate this Third Dutch War, by his action in sending out the ever-ready Captain Holmes to intercept the Dutch Smyrna fleet before war was declared. For James it was a period of great excitement as he prepared, once again, to play a leading part in the fortunes of the nation, this time in support of a policy even more sympathetic to his nature than the more purely commercial origins of the last Dutch War. After a break of seven years, he was again entrusted with command of the English fleet. This time his flagship was to be the hundred-gun *Prince*. As James led a combined Anglo-French fleet into the last naval battle of his life, his two former companions-in-arms, Turenne and Condé, crossed the Rhine and invaded the United Provinces. Who could have thought that these provinces would still be independent and united by the end of the year?

Once again both Dutch and English were determined to seek out each other's fleets and destroy them. But this time James was denied the glory of a real victory. His great battle with the Dutch at Sole Bay was drawn. It was marked in English minds by the apparent desertion, or unwillingness to fight, of their French allies, a fact eagerly noted by the growing body of public opinion which considered the French alliance to be a disastrous mistake. The fight between the English and the Dutch was as savage as any that the participants could remember. James himself, though he has been criticised for his tactics, could hardly be faulted for his courage. He fought the *Prince* until she was a floating hulk, transferred his flag to the *St Michael* until she nearly foundered with her hold full of water, and finally moved to the *London*. Public opinion once again acclaimed him as a hero, shamefully let down by his French allies. The fact remained however that, despite heavy losses, the Dutch battle fleet was still at sea, and the war, which people had thought would last a few weeks, was obviously going to be long drawn out. This conclusion was borne out even more strongly

LEFT Battle of Sole Bay, which took place on 28 May 1672, between the forces of the Dutch and the English, aided by the French. The Earl of Sandwich commanded the English fleet under the Duke of York, and lost his life when his flagship *The Royal James*, was blown up by Dutch fireships. This painting by Willem van de Velde shows the destruction of *The Royal James*.
OPPOSITE BELOW Edward Montague, 1st Earl of Sandwich, portrayed by Lely in about 1670.

when the desperate Dutch imposed on themselves the dictatorship of the young, vigorous, war-like Prince of Orange, after twenty-two years of government by an oligarchy of merchants led by the Grand Pensionary, De Witt. The Dutch now prepared to resist the French invasion with measures more drastic than any to which the cost and profit-conscious merchants would ever have consented.

Faced with a long war, Charles's house of cards collapsed. His French subsidies were not nearly enough to meet his debts, and the nearly bankrupt King was forced to go to Parliament for money. In the two years that followed, the whole policy of the secret Treaty of Dover vanished and the Cabal disintegrated. Parliament refused any supply unless Charles not only withdrew his Declaration of Indulgence, which they objected to both as a pro-papist measure and because the King had by-passed Parliament in declaring it, but also passed a Test Act so worded that only members of the Anglican Church could hold office.

RIGHT The first page of the Test Act of 1673, which forced James as a Catholic to resign all his offices, including that of Lord High Admiral.

THE
Eſtabliſht Teſt.

WHAT a Tempeſt ſhould we have had, if this Black *Italian* Cloud had broken over our Heads? Never was *Hurricane* ſo double charged, with Death and Deſtruction: It would certainly have Rain'd Fire and Faggots, and all Inſtruments of Cruelty, upon the Innocent Heads of Poor *Proteſtants.* But *GOD* have the Praiſe, That we are in hopes to ſee it not only Blow over, but that the Storm is likely to fall upon the Heads that raiſed it. Some of theſe treacherous Dealers, who have dealt ſo very treacherouſly with us, are already *fallen into the Pit which they had digged for Others,* and are enſnared in the miſ-

B   chievous

Charles, the most supple of Stuart kings, bowed to necessity, ignored the advice of James to maintain the Declaration of Indulgence even at the risk of civil war, and agreed. And that, after three years, was the end of Charles's scheme to settle the Catholic religion on England. For James it was not only a defeat of that Grand Design which he alone had supported blindly through all disappointments; it was also a personal tragedy, for the Test Act, though naturally general in its wording, was, to a considerable extent, aimed directly at himself. Now at last, his conscience forced him to bring his Catholicism right out into the open and he had to resign all his offices. No longer could he be Lord High Admiral. No longer could the former hero of the nation lead the English fleet into action.

A victorious Parliament was generous to the defeated King, and Charles was able to continue the war for another year. But as the months passed, and no conclusive victories were won, the body of public opinion in opposition to the war grew in strength, and, despite all the efforts of Charles's now discredited ministers, the last of the Anglo-Dutch Wars was brought to an end in February 1674 by the Treaty of Westminster – as inconclusive a piece of paper as had marked the ending of the previous two wars. Out with Charles's policy went his ministers. Clifford, like James, refused to take the Test and was thus debarred from public office, to die in mysterious circumstances in the following year. Buckingham and Ashley, now Earl of Shaftesbury, went into opposition. The discredited Arlington became the butt of the Court – anyone who wanted a cheap laugh put a black patch on his nose and strutted around – and eventually retired to the country. Lauderdale alone remained to hound the Scots. Out of the ruins of the Cabal came Thomas Osborne, Earl of Danby, a former henchman of Buckingham, to be the King's first minister. He represented the antithesis of the policy enshrined in the secret Treaty of Dover. He was an anti-French Anglican. But, on the other hand, he was a strong supporter of the Royal prerogative, and virtually the only minister in the whole reign who was capable of balancing the national budget.

This period of the early 1670s, that was dominated for James in public life by the rise and fall of his hopes for the Grand Design, was also of fundamental importance in his private life. In March 1671 his wife Anne died after a long period of poor

James's two daughters by Anne Hyde: both of them became queen of England.
LEFT Mary, aged ten, portrayed as Diana drawing her bow, followed by a greyhound. Painting by Peter Lely.

RIGHT Anne, aged about three or four, wearing a feathered cap and holding a great tit by a piece of string. Portrait by Peter Lely.

health. James, with his constant guilty conscience, must have been terrified to hear her last words – 'Duke, Duke, death is terrible, death is very terrible.' He did not mourn for long, however. There seems no doubt that he had loved and respected her deeply, but for reasons of State, as well as for his personal convenience, it was important that he marry again quickly. Charles's marriage with Catherine of Braganza was clearly never going to produce a child, and James, the next heir to the throne, had only female children, Mary and Anne, surviving

CONVERTE ANGLIAM

It is a foolish Sheep that makes the Wolf her Confessor

from his first marriage. Charles was alarmed at the thought that James might once again make a fool of himself; he was a terrible one for falling in love. So one of James's closest friends, Lord Peterborough, was sent on a princess-hunting tour of Europe. Reports and portraits flowed in, but James could not make up his mind. One was too fat, another too ugly, yet another had red hair which he detested. At last, Peterborough, having been to half the Courts in Europe, found a really suitable match. Mary of Modena was a lovely girl of seventeen destined for the convent, who screamed for two days and nights when she was told that she was to be the bride, not of Christ, but of a forty-year-old duke in a country she had never heard of. But 'the ladies of Italy', as Peterborough was told, 'have no will but that of their friends'. Mary had no choice but to do her duty as a princess. And, on 21 November 1673, her husband noted that the Princess Mary of Modena 'had arrived at Dover and had been wedded and bedded that same night'.

The tall, dark, beautiful Princess was to prove a brave and loyal wife to James, but her devotion to her religion and her unwillingness or incapacity to understand English society and institutions were to contribute to his downfall. The girlish grace which charmed her first English admirers was to undergo change in the climate of her new home. Those eyes which Peterborough had found 'so full of light and sweetness' were later to flash with jealousy and bad temper and to look upon her subjects with haughtiness and disdain. But for the moment they were just full of tears.

Public opinion in England was appalled that the now declared Papist heir to the throne should openly marry an Italian princess, who was quite clearly the Pope's eldest daughter. Catholic opinion abroad thought that a pretty young wife might do something to temper the Duke's remorseless urge to commit adultery. This, however, was rather optimistic. James himself was delighted with his wife, and thought she would make a pleasant playmate for his eleven-year-old daughter, Mary. The new Duchess, once installed at St James's Palace, cheered up quite quickly. James, she wrote, 'has the holy fear of God and is very kind to me. He is so firm and steady in our holy religion.' Indeed he was – far too firm and steady for the English people.

OPPOSITE James's marriage in 1673 to the Catholic Princess Mary of Modena, caused great consternation in England. She was regarded by many as the Pope's eldest daughter, and her Catholic confessor Father Edward Petre was clearly a wolf.

M^r. EDWARD COLEMAN *as he was drawne*
For high Treafon againft his Maties *sacred Pe*
Proteftant Religion, and

5 A Papist at Bay
1673-85

sledge to Execution December 4.ᵗʰ 1678.
v. And endeavouring the Alteration of the
bvertion of the Governmᵗ.

with Allowance.

THE FAILURE OF the policy enshrined in the Secret Treaty of Dover and the disappointments of the Third Dutch War made no difference to James's ambitions. He continued to regard the Grand Design, the settling of the Catholic religion on England, as his life-work. He remained on the extreme right of English politics, the strongest supporter of a French alliance, of the King's rights to unfettered use of his prerogative and of the Catholic religion. As Charles, the realist, moved away from these extreme positions, he did so only after having endured tireless criticism and pressure from his unrelenting brother, who refused to remember the good sense of what he had learned in his military days under Turenne – the sound policy of a tactical withdrawal from an extreme and exposed position. James remained a tactless and obstinate man who could see no right in any view but his own. It was fortunate for Charles that his brother had sufficient restraint not to scream the secret clauses of the Treaty of Dover from the roof of St James's Palace. James never revealed the terms of the Treaty and Charles retained his Crown, but nonetheless James continued his work of forwarding the Grand Design. He did this at two levels.

In public, he formed one of a triumvirate with Danby and Lauderdale, which took the place of the now disintegrated Cabal. Both Danby and Lauderdale were firm believers in a strong monarchy, but both were also Protestants and knew nothing of their master's former ambitions for the Catholic religion. Danby, whose talents included the ability to reorganise the royal finances, and to use such money to keep a sweet majority for the policies of the Court in the House of Commons, was the King's acknowledged first minister. He very soon found himself in an extremely embarrassing position. The main issue in the years following the end of the Third Dutch War was what King Charles would do with the army he now had at his command. Would he use it once more in alliance with France to destroy the Dutch, or in alliance with the Dutch to check the ambitions of France? Or would he disband it? Charles wanted to keep his options open, and would commit himself to nothing, using his existing army to extract money from France, alarm Holland and threaten any of his unruly subjects who might be having disloyal thoughts about reducing the royal prerogative. Public opinion, as represented in Parliament, wanted the army

Thomas Osborne, Earl of Danby, Charles's chief minister following the break-up of the Cabal. Portrait by the studio of Lely.

either disbanded or used against France. And Danby, as the very soul of Anglican francophobia, supported public opinion on this point, but, as the good servant of a difficult master, was forced to concur in Charles's secret dealings with Louis XIV, to the point of actually being the channel by which French money was brought into England. The discovery of Danby's double-dealings was to lead to his downfall, but before then he had much success in encouraging Charles to move to the left, despite the powerful opposition of James. The laws against the Catholics were tightened up during these years, and no doubt many of the old religion followed William Blundell's example of burying his altar stone beneath the pantry window. And Danby's outward pro-Dutch policy was carried to a remarkable conclusion by the marriage of the Stadholder hero William of Orange to James's own daughter, Mary, in 1677. Despite the fact that both her parents became Catholic converts after her birth, Mary had remained a Protestant and the marriage was hailed in England as a triumph for the Protestant and pro-Dutch majority. James had naturally opposed the marriage. He had in fact tried to arrange a match with Louis XIV's son, the Dauphin; one can imagine the uproar that would have followed had he succeeded. Knowing he was beaten, James accepted William of Orange, and his enormous correspondence with his son-in-law during the next eleven years illustrates both his wish to remain on good terms with him and his failure to realise the unfilial ambitions of that rather unpleasant, but very talented man.

If James was disappointed by his brother's failure to stem the general movement to the left in English politics during these years, he had no better fortune in his private schemes to advance the Royalist, Catholic cause. The main evidence we have for James's activities as a secret schemer is the correspondence of his secretary, Edward Coleman, which was to be exposed in dramatic circumstances some years later. Coleman, vain and somewhat unrealistic like his master, was a Catholic convert who had been educated by the Jesuits. Over two hundred letters of his correspondence with such people as Père la Chaise, Louis XIV's Jesuit confessor, the papal nuncio at Brussels and the English Cardinal Howard at the papal Court, survive. The letters – obscure, usually coded and sometimes written in lemon juice between the lines – expose in guarded terms Coleman's ambitions to forward the Catholic religion in England. His main aim was to obtain papal or French money, either to enable the King to rule without Parliament, or for the wholesale bribing of both the Lords and Commons. Following this start, his scheme was to declare for general religious toleration in the country, and then to replace Protestants by Catholics in the key positions in the State, until eventually, by force and example, the Catholic religion would once more be settled on England. The whole business was given an urgency and expectation of success by the fact that James, the heir to the throne, was such a strong supporter of the Catholic cause. 'God has given us a prince who is become (may I say, a miracle) zealous of being the author and instrument of so glorious a work.' Coleman's opinion of the King reflects a common and, as it turned out, totally inaccurate assessment of Charles. Believing that he was entirely devoted to his pleasures and wanted nothing but a quiet life, he wrote: 'the duke would be able to govern him without trouble, and mark out to him what he ought to do for the establishment of his grandeur and repose'.

Some writers have assumed that Coleman, certainly a born intriguer, was acting on his own, and that James was not privy to this correspondence. This seems most unlikely. It would naturally have been very dangerous for James to act as a principal at this stage, hence the use of Coleman and King Louis's confessor as intermediaries. But James must have known of the letters, and that he felt Coleman to be an essential person to have in his household is shown by the fact that, though he was twice forced to dismiss him, each time Coleman was quickly reinstalled, as either James's or his wife's secretary. Perhaps more to the point, the policy outlined by Coleman was almost exactly the policy which James was to adopt some ten years later when he came to the throne.

Coleman had no success in his intriguing. Though both the Pope and Louis XIV were interested in his schemes, neither felt that they had sufficient chance of success to spend money on, and indeed had considerable doubts that any money handed over would in fact be spent on the settling of the Catholic religion. One of Coleman's replies may have reinforced such doubts: 'Logic built upon money has more charms at the Court

'God has given us a prince who is become . . . zealous of being the author and instrument of so glorious a work'

of St James than any other form of reasoning.' The English were known to be greedy, even if James was sincere. And was he in any case prepared to implicate himself in this design? There was little sign that he was yet ready to go to such lengths, and, until he was, there would be no money. It was expensive enough trying to keep Charles neutral, without putting his brother and large numbers of Catholic lords on the French pay-roll as well.

While Coleman intrigued, the strength of the opposition to the Court generally, and the royal brothers in particular, was growing. Shaftesbury, with his genius for controlling men, was slowly welding all the various groups of critics into one powerful weapon. The main strength of this weapon was to be the traditional opponents of the Stuarts – country gentlemen, who, from lack of inclination or good fortune, enjoyed none of the perks of being a courtier. Such men were the heirs of the middle party of the early 1640s, and now were agreed on their dislike of the corruption of the Court, the Catholic religion, the expense and danger of a standing army and the power of France. But Shaftesbury's connections went beyond his own class. To the left of the country party lay all those groups who had descended into political limbo since the Restoration. Such were the Presbyterians and old Cromwellians of the 1650s who had never sold themselves to the Anglican reaction or, even further to the left, radicals and republicans, whose strength lay in the artisan class of London, and who could be transformed by a demagogue of Shaftesbury's ability into 'brisk boys', with boots large enough to persuade wavering Parliamentarians where their best interest lay. On the right, Shaftesbury could find support among disappointed courtiers, the 'outs' who hoped to get back 'in' by opposition rather than flattery. Among this group there were a growing number who were backing a dark and very attractive horse who appeared to be making ground rapidly. This was King Charles's favourite bastard son, James Scott, Duke of Monmouth, already, with his good looks and easy-going habits, a popular hero who felt he would make an appealing Prince of Wales.

Shaftesbury courted and flattered all these groups, paring away at their disparate hates and ambitions, until he had combined them all in pursuit of one objective, an objective which seemed to all of them the first step in getting what they wanted – the prevention of that bigoted papist James, Duke of York, from ever becoming King of England. Reasons to hate and fear the heir to the throne were not difficult to find. To the Court he was the gloomy, moralising convert who tried to spoil their fun. To the country he was the most extreme advocate of the pro-French and pro-Catholic policies which they so hated. And what was he to his brother whose consent would be necessary if he was to be excluded from the succession? Charles had repeatedly made clear his views on the sanctity of hereditary succession. He had refused to divorce his barren wife in order to breed a legitimate child. He had refused to underwrite the story that he had married Lucy Walters, Monmouth's mother, in France. There was, therefore, no doubt that Charles regarded James as his heir. But he often seemed to show a dislike of James in public, which encouraged people to think that he might be prepared to disinherit his brother if put under sufficient pressure. As so often, public opinion underestimated Charles's strength of character. Whether he loved him or not, he stuck to his brother to the end. Indeed, brotherly affection hardly entered the question. Charles recognised that if he could be forced to desert his brother, the same forces could destroy the royal prerogative, as he knew it, for ever.

As the forces of opposition gathered their strength, the man who was to be the catalyst of their struggle against the King was preparing his own Grand Design. The extraordinary figure of Titus Oates was about to burst onto the stage of English history. The hideous Oates, his moon-face almost bisected by an enormous mouth, entered the English Jesuit college at St Omer in December 1677. Six months later he was expelled, hardly an unusual experience for Oates, who had been expelled from most institutions to which fate had introduced him, including what must have required something of a genius for unparsonly behaviour – a chaplaincy in the Royal Navy. But six months at St Omer, the most distinguished of the large number of English Jesuit colleges on the Continent, was sufficient for Oates to get the names and whereabouts of most of the leading Catholics and Jesuit priests at that time in England. With this information his fertile imagination was able to concoct a detailed Popish Plot, designed to titivate all the prejudices and fears of an hysterical Protestant nation. The Society of Jesus, encouraged and

The Popish Plot

The Popish Plot was concocted in the fertile mind of Titus Oates. He was expelled in December 1673 from the Jesuit seminary of St Omer, but had obtained during his stay the names and whereabouts of many leading Catholics and Jesuit priests in England. Armed with this information he declared that the Society of Jesus, financed by the Pope and Louis XIV, was planning to murder Charles II and put James on the throne. Belief in the reality of the plot caused hysteria throughout the country.

RIGHT Satire of 1681 referring to the Popish Plot. Below, the infernal conclave of the Pope and his supporters plots to murder Charles, while above, Titus Oates and Charles are depicted as the happy instruments of England's salvation.

Pickerin Executed.

S.r William waller burning Popish books, Images, and Relicques.

ABOVE In May 1685, soon after James's succession to the throne, Titus Oates was indicted for perjury and found guilty. He received a severe sentence of imprisonment with floggings, and was put in the pillory outside Westminster Hall. Painting after Jan Wyck.

LEFT Delftware tiles showing various episodes in the Popish Plot.

Behold Two Crafty Iesuits fighting,
Only to draw a Zealous Knight in.

Whom striving to apease their brangle,
That weak Old man does basely strangle.

Tis strange though how his joynts are bended,
In Chair; and then againe extended.

Our Towns They burn our goods they plunder,
By such sly tricks, twill make you wonder.

Povis might hope to mend his fortune,
What Staffords end was, we are certain.

Their Chancelor nere studied Law,
Their Major General Campe nere saw.

See how they veiw him with delight,
Whilst Lady's dance and Pisspot spright.

By watchful sentrie th'are not seen,
For th'Devil thrusts his Paw between.

ut wonder more how they durst venture,
For killing King, to signe Indenture.

Behold their Generall, a stout Tory,
Peters ayme was only Glory.

The pious Pilgrims inclination,
Was to pervert and damn this Nation.

And Irish Tory with black Bull,
Wou'd kill us all, if we sit still.

financed by the Pope and Louis XIV, were planning to murder Charles and put James on the throne. They were to be supported in this conspiracy by troops raised by the Catholic nobility, assisted by large contingents from France and Ireland. Once they were in control of the country, the Protestant religion was to be suppressed. Imaginary plots of this sort were common gossip in the seventeenth century, and Charles's first reaction was to treat Oates, who was easily detected in straight lies and constantly contradicted himself, with the derision he deserved. This would clearly have been the best thing to do. But neither Danby, James nor Oates himself would let the King do it. James, who must have felt the whole thing to be a little close to the bone, and who was much disturbed at himself being named as the figurehead of the plot, insisted on a full public enquiry to clear his name. Danby, already alarmed at having been forced into secret dealings with France, was not going to give his opponents the chance of accusing him of hushing up the knowledge of a projected Catholic rebellion. And Oates, whose main motives seem to have been greed and love of the limelight, was not going to have his fantasy thrust aside. Doubtful of the sincerity of the Privy Council's decision to make a full enquiry into the Plot, he left further copies of his deposition with a prominent London magistrate, Sir Edmund Berry Godfrey. Charles was forced to allow a full investigation into all of Oates's allegations.

The results were disastrous. In spite of Oates's obvious lies and contradictions and those of the numerous other informers who sprang up to join in the pickings, hysterical public opinion was prepared to believe in every detail of the Plot, and such opinion was well represented in the various legal bodies, including both Houses of Parliament, which investigated the case. Indeed, not to believe in the Plot was seen to be a sign that the doubter was at least a secret papist, and probably also an agent in the devilish work himself. Very soon the prisons were filling up with Catholic priests and prominent citizens who had been named by Oates or other perjurors. All the dormant hatred for Catholics was brought out into the open, the penal laws were fully enforced, and innocent papists were forced either to go quietly to ground until the storm had subsided or to flee the country. Public opinion was brought to fever heat by the murder of Godfrey, the magistrate with whom Oates had left his deposition. The murder has never been solved; but to popular opinion of the time it was clear that he had been murdered by the Catholics to keep his mouth shut. Soon, more informers appeared to name his murderers, and yet more innocents were clapped in irons in Newgate and the Tower. 'The credulous all over the kingdoms were terrified and affrighted with armies landing, of pilgrims, black bills, armies under ground and what not.' Parliament, remembering Guy Fawkes, searched its cellars, and an armed guard was sent to intercept any Jesuit explosives experts who might venture therein; women carried loaded pistols in their muffs; and the law-courts solemnly tried, convicted and sentenced to the hideous punishment for treason a number of Jesuit priests, as well as many less distinguished persons who had had the misfortune to be fingered for the murder of Godfrey. It is pleasing to learn that even in the midst of this mockery of justice, Pepys's clerk, Samuel Atkins, was found 'Not Guilty' of the murder of Godfrey, having established beyond all possible doubt that he had spent the relevant time drinking on a yacht at Greenwich. Few men had such unimpeachable alibis.

James, who had been so prominent in demanding the investigation of the Plot, was very nearly destroyed by it – not by Oates, who rather cleverly denied that James was concerned in it, but was only to be an unwilling and unknowing figurehead; no, James's problem was his Catholic secretary, Coleman. Coleman was a close friend of Godfrey and the latter was able to warn him, before his murder, that his name appeared among those of the ringleaders of the Plot. James also warned him. So it seems extraordinary that, when Coleman's rooms were searched on the order of Danby, he should have left anything to incriminate him. But he had. There, hidden in a secret recess behind his fireplace, was his indubitably treasonable correspondence. Coleman's letters gave the whole Plot a credibility it had lacked before. It was a superb piece of guesswork on Oates's part to name him. Or was it? A man who failed to destroy such evidence must have been amazingly vain and indiscreet – indiscreet enough to lead to gossip among the Jesuits at St Omer? We shall never know. Coleman, if a fool, was a brave and loyal one, and he never said a word against his

'The credulous all over the kingdoms were terrified and affrighted with armies landing, of pilgrims . . . and what not'

Design for a playing card of 1684, showing Edward Coleman –
James's Catholic secretary – being interrogated in
Newgate Gaol concerning his part in the Popish Plot.

master on the road to a traitor's death. He was probably the only victim of the Popish Plot who was in fact a traitor.

For Shaftesbury, the Popish Plot was an invaluable aid in his campaign to destroy the Duke of York. It could hardly have been better timed. For years, Danby, firm in his control of the Cavalier Parliament, had been able easily to circumvent the left-wing opposition, and to seize all the glory of anti-papist legislation. Until both he and the Parliament he managed so effectively had disappeared, Shaftesbury had little chance of pushing his policies to a successful conclusion. But now Shaftesbury was ready to play out one of his aces. Two months after Parliament re-assembled after the summer recess – two months of growing hysteria and excitement whipped up by the Whig leader – the former ambassador in Paris, Ralph Montagu, produced documentary evidence that Danby had made secret negotiations with Louis, and was in fact receiving a regular pension from that generous King. Danby, the Anglican friend of Holland, was on the French pay-roll. Four days later, a suitably indignant House of Commons, shocked no doubt by a French pensioner who had been so careless as to be found out, successfully impeached Danby for high treason. There was pained disbelief at Danby's counter-claim that several of the Whig leaders were also in French pay, and, although the Lords refused to commit Danby, he spent the next five years cooling his heels in the Tower, occasionally visited by a perplexed Charles with some financial problem on his mind. Charles, now thoroughly alarmed at what else Montagu might have been paid to say, prorogued, and then, on 24 January 1679, dissolved the eighteen-year-old Cavalier Parliament. It had lost some of its original loyalty and subservience to the Crown, but it was still more loyal than any other Parliament Charles was likely to get. Shaftesbury and his agents began to prepare the necessary persuasion and propaganda to ensure the election of a really hostile House of Commons.

James was to miss the excitement of the elections, for Charles had found him nothing but an embarrassment during the emotions of the Popish Plot. Apart from constantly telling him what to do, he provided a focus for popular hatred, a focus rather too near the Crown for Charles's liking. So James was sent off to Brussels for the duration of the troubles. Not that

The English Country House

Many great English country houses were built in the 1680s. Chatsworth was a Tudor house, built in the mid-sixteenth century by Bess of Hardwick, but by 1684, the fabric had become decayed and old-fashioned. William Cavendish, 4th Earl of Devonshire, who was a leading Whig politician of the period, called in William Talman to remodel the south and east fronts in 1684. As the building mania overtook him, Cavendish went on to remodel the west front with the help of an unknown architect, and finally the great curved north front was completed by Thomas Archer in 1707. The Tudor core of Chatsworth had been competely transformed to create one of the most magnificent houses of the age.

RIGHT The south front of Chatsworth, built by William Talman between 1684 and 1689. The Cavendish motto 'Cavendo Tutus' appears just below the cornice.

BELOW Kip and Knyff's engraving of c. 1700 of Chatsworth, from the south, with Talman's remodelled front facing, but the west and north fronts still retaining their Tudor character. The great Baroque formal gardens at Chatsworth were laid out by Henry Wise.

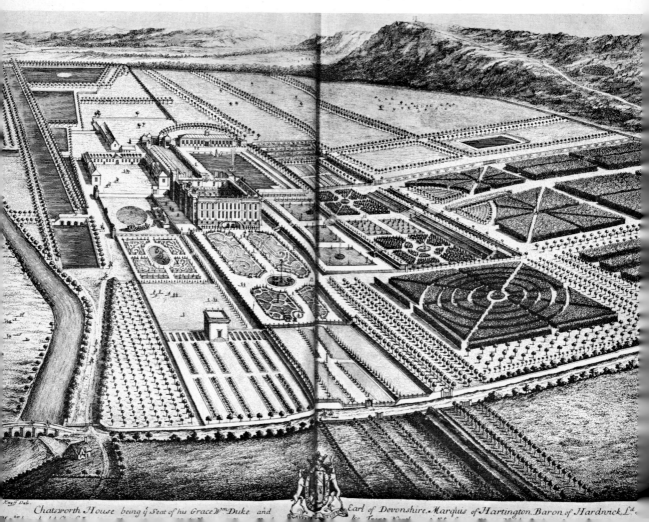

Chatsworth House being ÿ Seat of his Grace Wm Duke and Earl of Devonshire, Marquis of Hartington, Baron of Hardwick, Ld.

BELOW The west front of
Belton House in
Lincolnshire. The house
was built between 1684
and 1687 for a wealthy
lawyer, Sir John Brown.
It was modelled upon
Edward Hyde's great
London mansion,
Clarendon House,
Piccadilly, which had been
constructed to the designs
of Roger Pratt in 1664–7.

this kept him quiet. A constant stream of confidential messengers and messages flowed from the Spanish Netherlands to London. But letters were easier to ignore than James. It was thus a frustrated and rather bored James who looked about for something to pass the time. Luckily the stag-hunting was quite good and, as a short visit grew longer, James sent to the Master of his Foxhounds to bring his hounds and huntsmen over. James, confident in the ultimate defeat of his and his brother's opponents, had settled in.

With James out of the way, the battle for his future began in earnest. For the next three years Shaftesbury's campaign to whip up anti-papist feeling in the country, and get Parliament to pass an Act excluding the Catholic heir to the throne from the succession, dominates English history. In three successive Parliaments virtually nothing else was discussed. As time went on, the confident James of early 1679 became increasingly glum and despondent, and the advice which poured into his brother grew increasingly militant, for all the cards seemed to be in Shaftesbury's hands. Popular opinion against the Catholics in general, and James in particular, remained at fever heat, and the Whig leader had no difficulty in ensuring large majorities in successive Houses of Commons to vote for the exclusion of James.

That Shaftesbury lost the battle and was to die a broken man in exile, only some four years later, provides a fascinating object-lesson in seventeenth-century political reality. For the apparent unity of the opposition to James concealed serious flaws, which could easily be exploited by the Tories. The most obvious flaw was that a policy to exclude James presupposed the naming of another successor to Charles. Who was it to be, demanded the Tories. The Whigs, very much divided on this point, were embarrassed. The official line, embodied in the Exclusion Bills, was that the succession should pass as if James was in fact dead. In other words, it should pass to James's elder daughter, Mary, who was now, as we have seen, the wife of William III of Orange. But few of the Whigs were happy at the thought of the Dutch Stadholder as the effective ruler of England. He had a reputation for absolutism himself, and though indubitably a Protestant and anti-French, he was also at least half a Stuart, the son of James's sister and the husband of his daughter, and apparently on very good terms with both his English uncles. William himself bided his time, courting all factions, but never committing himself. As time went on, more of the Whigs focussed their attention on the other obvious candidate, the Duke of Monmouth. During the years 1679 and 1680 his popularity increased immensely. As Captain-General of the English army he had suppressed the Covenanters' rebellion in Scotland, showing at the same time military competence and leniency to the defeated rebels, with whom many of the left-wing Whigs sympathised. Since then, despite being removed from his command at the insistence of James and twice being ordered out of the country, he had done more or less as he pleased. He had made semi-royal progresses in the West Country and in the North, and his health had been drunk as Prince of Wales by adoring crowds who marvelled at his beauty, his sweet temper and his amazing athletic prowess. Horse-races, foot-races, stripped or in his boots, the beautiful bastard won them all. But bastard he was, and bastard, much as he loved him, his indulgent father intended him to remain. Any Whig support for Monmouth was therefore countered by massive opposition from the main body of the country gentlemen, terrified of what their own by-blows might claim if once the principle of legitimate succession, the only security of property, was thus cast aside. The apparent successes of Monmouth scared James, already jealous of his nephew for having been appointed Captain-General. But his cause was really always a lost cause, and served only to split the Whigs at a time when unity was essential.

'Our beloved Protestant Duke'

The Whigs were up against even greater problems than their inability to agree on a successor to Charles. They were up against the most striking political characteristic of that class from which they drew most of their strength, the deep-rooted conservatism of the English country gentleman. Such conservatism had two main principles. First, there was an almost instinctive belief in the nation at large that it should in the last resort be ruled by a king. Such a belief had been much strengthened by the continued memory of the shifts and unpleasantness of the Interregnum. Shaftesbury himself told Evelyn that he would support the principle of monarchy 'to his last breath, as having seen and felt the misery of being

under a mechanic tyranny'. Secondly, it was very generally agreed that the Crown, like private property, should descend by strict hereditary succession. To agree to the exclusion of James, it was felt, would be to make the monarchy elective, to reduce the King of England to the status of the King of Poland or the Doge of Venice, rulers of states whose constitutions were much despised by most contemporary Englishmen. Such beliefs led many who objected to James's Catholicism and his reputation for absolutism, to search for alternatives to his exclusion from the succession. One idea was to appoint William and Mary regents if James should ever succeed his brother. A more popular alternative was to enact in Parliament limitations on the prerogative powers of a Catholic king. The true Whigs ridiculed such suggestions. If James was to come to the throne, they said, he would simply ignore them. As it turned out, this was a very accurate assessment of how James was to behave as king, but, in the period of the exclusion crisis, limitations posed an attractive alternative for many opponents of James as a man. Indeed, there were many who felt that such limitations would never in fact have to be placed on a king, for it was widely

Edinburgh in the
seventeenth century,
from Slezer's *Theatrum
Scotiae*, 1693.

believed that Charles would outlive his brother. He was, after
all, only three years older, and had a reputation for athletic
endurance and extremely good health.

Such a reputation received a rude shock in August 1679, when
Charles suddenly fell ill and seemed likely to die. Moderates and
Tories alike were terrified that the Duke of Monmouth,
Captain-General of the forces, might seize the Crown in
James's absence. James was hurried back to England in the
thinnest of disguises, and rushed to the bedside of a fully-
recovered brother, who was much amused at the alarms and
hopes his illness had aroused. Deciding that life would be much
easier without either his beloved son or his selfless brother, he
ordered a General Post. James was sent to Scotland, and Monmouth to the Low Countries. Charles himself prepared for the
next round in his duel with Shaftesbury.

We have seen that Charles had much more going for him in
such a duel than might at first appear. Indeed it could be argued
that it was in fact impossible for a king, who knew how to play,
to lose such a duel. It is the tragedy of the dynasty that Charles II
was the only Stuart who was clever enough, or sufficiently

unscrupulous, to beat his opponents at their own game. For Charles was just as clever and just as elusive as that 'Dorsetshire eel', the first Earl of Shaftesbury, who opposed him. Charles knew that he had sufficient strength to win all the rounds that really mattered in a match that seemed to many contemporaries a lost cause. Thanks to the ability of Danby, he had a much larger income now than at the beginning of his reign, an income which he felt sure he could swell in time of need by extracting further subsidies from France. He alone had the power to prorogue or dissolve Parliament when he wanted to, and an opponent like Shaftesbury was powerless without the organised forum of Parliament. It was at his pleasure that the judges, the most powerful arm of the executive, held their offices, and he knew that such judges would do all within their power to secure verdicts favourable to their royal master. Finally, he was able to play on the division amongst the Whigs and the strong tradition of loyalty to the Crown in the country as a whole, and especially in the House of Lords, to break up the solid phalanx of the opposition.

With so much on Charles's side, it is a tribute to the genius of Shaftesbury and an indication of the hatred felt for James that the Whigs came so close to winning the struggle. Time and time again James, feeling the Parliamentary battle lost, urged his brother to force the contest into a wider arena and decide the issue with the sword – the swords of loyal Irishmen and Scotsmen, paid with the money of Louis XIV, now thoroughly alarmed at the prospect of England descending for the second time in forty years into a republic. How much more subtle were the tactics that Charles actually employed. By appointing leaders of the Whig opposition to sit on his Council, he successfully alienated them from their followers, who saw their acceptance of such posts as evidence of time-serving. By agreeing, or pretending to agree, to limitations on the prerogative of a Popish successor, he gained the support of much moderate opinion, frightened in any case by the imminent prospect of civil war. By successive prorogations and dissolutions of Parliament, he removed the floor from under his opponents' feet whenever things looked particularly dangerous. These policies also prolonged the crisis to such an extent that opposition concentration on the one issue and the repetitive propaganda became so stale and boring that many people lost interest, and an almost inevitable reaction to the Whig hysteria set in. And then finally, when assured of his strength in the country, and secure in the prospect of more French money from yet another secret treaty, he dissolved the third and last of the crisis Parliaments at Oxford in March 1681. Though nobody knew it at the time, this was the greatest victory for the Crown in that whole long war between Stuart kings and their gentlemen subjects in Parliament which dominates the history of seventeenth-century England. The Tory reaction had begun, and Charles never had to summon another Parliament.

All this was far too clever for James. Partly because he was not involved in much of the day-to-day business of the crisis, but mainly because he was far too narrow-minded to appreciate the subtlety of his brother, he learned nothing from the crisis, or rather, what he did learn were the wrong lessons. His letters constantly begged Charles to be firm, to give no ground or all would be lost, whereas the truth was that all might well have been lost if Charles had been firm at the wrong time like his father. Giving ground and making false promises seemed weak to James, a man of resolution who prided himself on keeping his word. It was also dishonest by any standard but that of politics. But it was effective. James never learned that lesson. He was to think that it was always possible for a king to hold his own against his subjects, whatever his policy, so that, when he was eventually forced to retreat, his fall was headlong. Another lesson of the crisis that James failed to learn was that the world is not divided into two groups only, the left and the right. He failed to understand that contemporary politics, like contemporary religion, was a spectrum and not two distinct colours. For instance, he never understood Halifax, the Great Trimmer, who shifted the weight of his oratory from one side to another in order to maintain some semblance of moderation. James was naturally pleased to hear of Halifax's great speech which helped to persuade the Lords to vote against the Exclusion Bill, but was perplexed to hear the next day that the same Halifax had proposed limitations on a Popish king's prerogative powers, and had even suggested James's banishment. Where did the man stand? James felt that all England should be either for him or against him. He never appreciated two important political truths – the enormous reservoir of loyalty represented by moderate opinion, and the fact that even this reservoir had its limits.

Much of what James did learn during these crisis years he learned in Scotland. James had no particular love for the Scottish people, but he found the country itself much to his taste. He missed his favourite sport of stag-hunting, it is true, 'for where the stags are there are such hills and bogs as 'tis impossible to follow any hounds', but there were grouse to be shot and golf to be played as a consolation for a Prince who hated to be cooped up indoors. And, in more serious matters, Scotland was a paradise compared to impertinent England. The contrast was obvious the moment he crossed the border. After a long journey up the Great North Road where dislike of him and what he stood for was scarcely concealed, his progress from Berwick to Edinburgh was a real triumph. Two thousand of the nobility and gentry turned out to welcome him and his young Duchess, and, when he arrived in Edinburgh, 'the cannons of the castle went off for a considerable time, and bonfires were made throughout all the town and the ringing of the bells continued until ten o'clock at night'. He can hardly have encountered such enthusiasm since his return from the Battle of Lowestoft in 1665. His pleasure at this unexpected popularity was increased when he discovered more about the political system of the northern kingdom. For, since the Restoration, Scotland had been turned into an absolutist's dream in comparison with England.

Beneath the air of Gothic unreality, the mountains and the mist, the Highland chieftains feuding with each other in remote areas where the King's writ did not even pretend to run, a witch-ridden people sunk in terrible poverty had been dragooned into a humbled nation, ruled for the most part by a small committee who sat normally some four hundred miles away in London. There was no Parliamentary opposition here. As the Lord Advocate remarked, 'if the burghs had liberty to choose whom they pleased to represent them, factious and disloyal persons might prevail to get themselves elected'. Nor did the loyal persons who sat in the Scottish Parliament have any choice in the matters to which they were dictated to assent. Such matters were chosen by a body known as the Lords of the

Articles, themselves under the control of the Crown. The process was explained by Lauderdale, as Secretary of State for Scotland, the main architect of this repressive system: 'Nothing can come to parliament but through the Articles, and nothing can pass in the Articles but what is warranted by His Majesty, so that the King is absolute master in parliament both of the negative and affirmative.' There were thus few problems for the Scottish Privy Council, who could, if they wished, raise a large army at the expense of the Scottish tax-payers, not only to control their potentially rebellious fellow-countrymen, but also to threaten England. Few men, least of all James, had forgotten where Monck had come from twenty years before. On James's first visit to Scotland he was a very interested observer of the Scottish scene, and digested lessons on the management of kingdoms far more palatable than those his brother was teaching him in London. On his second visit, from October 1680 to May 1682, he replaced the unpopular Lauderdale as the virtual ruler of the northern kingdom, and was able to apply in practice the lessons he had learned.

Scotland, which had been the arbiter of English affairs on many occasions between Charles I's unwise attempt to impose the Anglican prayer-book in 1637 and the Restoration, was now, as we have seen, an apparently loyal and obedient nation. Although the reimposed episcopacy lay somewhat uneasily on a Presbyterian people, the only real signs of the militant Calvinism of the earlier period lay in the south-west of the kingdom. Here lived the Covenanters, or Cargillites as they were sometimes called, a body of people who had remained in almost constant rebellion against the Stuarts ever since the Restoration. They claimed to be the only people still faithful to the Solemn League and Covenant of 1638, representatives of the fanaticism and physical and moral courage which had characterised the Scots and Parliamentary armies in the Civil Wars. Since the Covenanters refused to accept any government that did not share their beliefs, and seemed only too happy to give their lives for those beliefs, they posed a difficult problem for their rulers. They could only be exterminated or tolerated, but toleration of such people was an impossibility for any government with pretensions to absolute rule. Lauderdale, during his long rule of Scotland, had treated them mercilessly, and had enforced to

'The King is absolute master in parliament both of the negative and affirmative'

133

the best of his skill the many savage laws enacted against them. His main agents in this policy of repression were Scots mercenaries, whose last employment had been in doing a similar job against recalcitrant subjects of the Tsar of Russia. The year before James's first visit to Scotland the now desperate Covenanters had been badly defeated in battle by Monmouth, but they still remained obstinately undeterred in their eternal revolt, encouraged from 1680 onwards by some of the English Whigs, who dreamed of their playing a role in English politics similar to that of the Army of the Covenant in 1638. James has been accused of savage and cruel treatment of these rebels during his second stay in Scotland, but this is probably unfair. Indeed, considering James's known views of both Calvinists and rebels, he showed a remarkable humanity. He continued Lauderdale's policy of trying to suppress the revolt, and he continued to a certain extent to use Lauderdale's methods, including judicial torture. But many witnesses, normally hostile to James, emphasise his leniency compared with previous rulers in Scotland. The real trouble was that James was up against people who were as fanatical in their beliefs as himself. James offered to pardon rebels captured in arms if they would say 'God save the King'. But to the really ardent rebels this was an impossible thing to say, just as it would have been impossible for James to take the Test. They would never ask their God to save this King. It was a hopeless situation.

Within the scope of the Scottish constitution as it then stood, there was naturally much importance attached to the character of the man who directed it. He had the power to make life extremely unpleasant for the people he ruled. On this score James's record in Scotland is very good. Despite his religion, he seems to have been very popular, and was much praised for the fairness of his rule. Being above Scottish politics, he was able to exercise the functions of an impartial umpire in smoothing out some of the more bitter arguments between the Scottish noblemen who helped him rule. His only really serious mistake was to turn the most powerful of all Scottish noblemen into an implacable enemy. Egged on by the Earl's many enemies, James agreed to charge the Earl of Argyll, head of the mighty Campbell clan, with treason, the evidence for which was patently weak. Whatever we may think of judicial murder

Carving of Arthur Capel, Earl of Essex, who was implicated in the Rye House Plot and committed suicide in his cell. Limewood carving by Grinling Gibbons.

today, it was in the seventeenth century an accepted weapon of the executive, and judges nearly always managed to square their consciences with the wishes of their masters. A packed court had no difficulty in finding Argyll guilty on evidence which, as Halifax remarked, would not have hanged a dog in England. But judicial murder, to be effective, needs to end in the death of the victim. James always insisted that he did not really intend to let Argyll be executed, only to keep him out of the way. Whether this was true or not, it was of course not known to the prisoner, and to let Argyll escape, and thus form another focus of opposition to the Stuarts, was a very silly thing to do. That James was indeed a silly man was clear to at least one shrewd Scotsman: 'Some wise men observed that the Duke of York might have honesty, justice and courage enough, and his father's peremptoriness, but that he had neither great conduct nor a deep reach in affairs, but was a silly man.'

135

On 5 February 1685, it was clear that Charles II was dying. James called for the Roman Catholic priest, Father John Huddlestone – who had first met Charles after the Battle of Worcester – to be smuggled into the King's bedroom. The King called out to him 'You that have saved my body, is now come to save my soul', and declared that he wished to die in the faith and communion of the Roman Catholic Church. Portrait of Father Huddlestone by Jacob Huysmans.

In March 1682 James at last returned to London to share in the reaction following his brother's triumph over the Whigs. What had once been a party apparently capable of dictating terms to the King had now totally disintegrated. James, who, only a few months before, had had no friends in England, found himself welcomed and fêted wherever he went. As for the Whig leaders, no one now had a good word for them, and within eighteen months most of them had disappeared for ever from the political scene. Shaftesbury died in exile; Russell and Sidney died traitors' deaths for their supposed part in the Rye House Plot – a conspiracy to assassinate the royal brothers on their way home from Newmarket in June 1683 – which was used as the basis of a rigged trial of Whig leaders in the same way that the Popish Plot was used against Catholics a few years earlier. But one should be careful not to exaggerate the bloodshed, either resulting from the Popish Plot or from the reactionary aftermath. Less than thirty people were executed in all, and apparently not a single person was killed in a riot, a remarkable indication of the basic saneness and dislike of violence which lay behind the public hysteria. James himself was disappointed at the mildness of the reaction, and consoled himself by some petty and rather unprincely suits for libel against people who had particularly annoyed him.

In the Tory reaction, James, as the greatest Tory of all, the man who had never wavered, recovered not only his popularity, but also his power in the State. For the last three years of the reign it was James and not Charles who did most of the ruling. King Louis, who had always had a high opinion of James and shared the common opinion that Charles was a lightweight, was delighted to see the Catholic Duke of York back in favour. 'The King of England could have taken no resolution more agreeable to his prosperity and reputation than that of re-establishing the Duke of York in all his offices.' The Test Act was forgotten. James was restored to the Privy Council, reinstated in all but name as Lord High Admiral, and became a member of the most important committees. Together with Pepys, he once more set about the reorganisation of the navy which in his absence had again fallen into disrepair. But James's main post was at his brother's side, anticipating or dictating his wishes, and saving him an immense amount of trouble. And indeed what harm could the haughty James do now in the world of Toryism? Charles had been proclaimed King in 1649, the nadir of the English monarchy. When he died suddenly thirty-six years later, he seemed to have defeated everything that the Civil War and the Interregnum had stood for. He was an absolute king ruling his pathetically loyal country without the aid of Parliament, but with the aid of French subsidies to help pay for his small standing army. James was eager to follow where his brother had led. But how would even a Tory nation take to a Catholic king who had learned his political lessons, not in England, but in Scotland and France?

6 King of the Tories 1685-8

WHAT A STRANGE DECADE in English history is the 1680s, and what a fickle thing, public opinion! Could they really be the same people who howled for James's exclusion from the succession in 1681, welcomed him as king in 1685, and yet were overjoyed at his deposition in 1688? It is the peculiar genius of James that in less than four years as sovereign he completely undermined the confidence of the most loyal and subservient people faced by an English king in the seventeenth century. It would have seemed inconceivable in 1650 that there should ever again be a King of England so absolutely secure as Charles was at the time of his unexpected death in February 1685. It would have seemed equally inconceivable in 1685 that one man could ever have destroyed that position of security as quickly as did James.

James at the age of fifty-one seemed to many the model of a Tory king. Few were blind to his faults, but his positive qualities seemed to more than outweigh them. It was on these qualities that the Tory nation of 1685 fixed their attention. His sobriety was contrasted with his brother's debauchery, his passion for work and his love of detailed administration with Charles's indifference and laziness, his honesty and loyalty with Charles's double-dealing. From the difficult years through which the nation had so recently passed, James now stood out as the champion of monarchy and property, the man who had never wavered, the ideal king of an Anglican, Tory nation. There was of course one problem. One of the most obvious things about James, and one which he made no attempt to conceal, was that he was not an Anglican. But the new King soon allayed any fears that this fact might have aroused. Shortly after his accession he told an eager nation that he intended to preserve the government 'in Church and State, as it is now by law established. I know the principles of the Church of England are for monarchy and the members of it have shewed themselves good and loyal subjects, therefore I shall always take care to defend and support it.' A Catholic king, famous above all else for keeping his word, would defend an Anglican nation.

That James was not the Tory stereotype his wishful-thinking supporters supposed him to be will be clear from what follows. On the other hand it is difficult, without using too much hindsight, to say exactly what he was. Certainly his religion was central to his behaviour, and his coterie of priests and his now mature Italian wife made certain that he was to think it more important to be a good Catholic than a good king. It seems clear, too, that the death of his brother removed a powerful restraint on his behaviour. James had always been haughty and single-minded in his pursuit of what he considered the right ends, but in the last resort, he had always bowed to Charles's decisions. Now, as king, he no longer had to, and he was not the sort of man who would listen to unwelcome advice from anyone else. It is not difficult to imagine the effect of the removal of such a restraint on a man whose ambitions for forwarding the Catholic religion and whose policy of firm dealing with opponents had been so constantly brushed aside by his subtle brother.

Nor was there anyone to replace Charles as a check on James's behaviour. The people whose opinion he most respected were just those, such as his wife and his priests, who urged him along the road to disaster. None of his personal friends, whether Protestant or Catholic, had much influence on him in really serious matters, though he expected total loyalty from them whatever he might do. Some of these friends had survived right through from the days of exile in France. Such was the Irish Catholic Dick Talbot, soldier of fortune, duellist and gamester, one of the young bloods who had sworn to Anne Hyde's lack of morals in 1660. Now Earl of Tyrconnel, he was soon to become the chief instrument of James's policies and his own ambition in Ireland. Another Catholic friend from the old days was the tiny fop, Harry Jermyn the younger, now created the first Baron Dover, and soon to take his seat on the Privy Council. A new generation of James's friends was represented by two staunch Protestants who had been in James's household since their early youth, and whose relationship to their now royal master was almost as son to father. We have already met John Churchill, the brother of James's mistress, now a baron, and already enjoying a reputation as a soldier of great talent. The career of George Legge, Lord Dartmouth, was very similar, though he was a lightweight compared with Churchill. Where the latter had grown up a soldier, Dartmouth was a sailor, but both had constantly been active in the Duke of York's interest during the troubled years of the Exclusion Crisis, and now

hoped for reward for their good service. While in Scotland, James had made some new friends who also hoped to exploit their influence on the King to forward their careers. Foremost among these were the Drummond brothers, two very ambitious men in their late thirties, soon to be the Earls of Perth and Melfort. Both decided that their careers would move forward faster under James if they apostasised, and they became Catholic converts in the second year of James's reign. The proud Perth, famous for his talent in telling a good story, was to be James's chief agent in Scotland, while the tall, dark, handsome Melfort acted as Scots Secretary in London, where he was able to exploit his charms to his best advantage on both the King and the Queen. Of all his personal friends, it was the extremist and

ABOVE The Drummond brothers, who became friends of James during his sojourn in Scotland. LEFT James, 4th Earl and 1st Duke of Perth, who was appointed James's chief agent in Scotland after his accession. RIGHT John, 1st Earl of Melfort, who acted as the Scottish Secretary in London and thus had a strong influence over the King.

unscrupulous Melfort who had most influence on James, and it is a sad indication of his inability to listen to what he did not wish to hear that he paid less attention to another of his Scottish friends, the Earl of Middleton. Charles, second Earl of Middleton, 'one of the pleasantest companions in the world', was a Protestant with a moderate Tory view of politics who could have done James much good.

If James's friends were either bad for him, or else gave good advice which was not listened to, the same could be said of the ministers whom he retained from his brother's reign. Chief among these were Robert Spencer, Earl of Sunderland, James's two brothers-in-law by his first marriage, the Earls of Rochester and Clarendon, and that great trimmer, the Marquess of Halifax. Sunderland, who rapidly manœuvred himself into the position of first minister, was a particularly disastrous choice for James. An inveterate gambler, both in politics and on the gaming tables, Sunderland's main interest was to stay in power and avoid the mistakes which he had made in the past. The man who had attached himself to both Arlington and Danby just before their falls, had eventually voted for Exclusion, and still found himself in favour was clearly a most accomplished politician. Both in his knowledge of foreign affairs and in his ability to manage Court and Parliament, he was invaluable, but he was not the man to try to deflect his master from the course he was set on. On the contrary, having gambled on James, he did everything he could to forward what he assumed, normally correctly, to be James's aims. Sunderland had virtually no religious convictions, and his ideal of right-wing government was that bureaucratic type of despotism now being brought to perfection by the ministers of Louis XIV. His main opponent in James's councils, Lawrence Hyde, Earl of Rochester, James's hard-drinking, hot tempered brother-in-law, who swore like a trooper in his cups, was a very different sort of right-wing politician. In many ways he was similar to the still discredited Danby. Both he and his brother represented the good old Anglican Tory ideals of their father and, as such, mirrored the mood of the nation at James's accession. Their uncompromising belief in the soundness of the Anglican religion and resistance to James's Catholicism was to end in their dismissal, despite their close relationship to the King. All James's ministers and friends

ABOVE George Savile, Marquess of Halifax, who was known as 'The Great Trimmer' because of his timely political *voltes-face*. Portrait of *c.* 1674–6, attributed to Mary Beale.

were to find that they were expected to do what he wanted them to do, or go. As we have already seen, he did not believe in compromise.

Despite his age and his new responsibilities, James made few changes in his private life when he became King. He continued to be a great figure in the hunting field, and could still outride his lords and keep 'pretty near the dogs, though the ditches were broad and deep, the hedges high, and the way and fields dirty and deep'. A succession of women could be seen by discerning eyes creeping up the backstairs of the palace, to disturb James's conscience and upset his devoted wife. Try as he might to be a good Catholic, he could not control himself. Arabella Churchill had been replaced as James's chief mistress by the plain and sensible Catherine Sedley, daughter of the Restoration poet and rake Sir Charles Sedley. A Protestant like her predecessor, she has earned a reputation as a wit, almost entirely on the evidence of one mocking remark in which she confessed her amazement at James's devotion: 'It cannot be my beauty because I haven't any, and it cannot be my wit because he hasn't enough of it himself to know that I have any.' At his succession she was barred from the palace by the King in an attempt to reform his behaviour, but she was soon back, to the alarm of James's priests whom she took pleasure in ridiculing and who feared that her Protestantism might influence their master. But they had no real cause for alarm. It is probable that James chose Protestant mistresses for the same reason that Charles suggested he chose ugly ones, and there is no evidence that Catherine talked either politics or religion in bed.

The country which James was destined to rule for so short a time had changed very considerably since he was a boy. Already the stereotype of the well-fed, beef-eating, beer-drinking Englishman was beginning to emerge, to be compared favourably with the starveling subjects of other nations. This was a somewhat misleading stereotype, since most Englishmen still lived in conditions of extreme poverty, but yet a reflection of a very real improvement in the main occupation of the people, agriculture, which had turned England from a grain-importing to a grain-exporting country in the course of the century, despite a rise in population. And for most of the

The Atchivement of a
tooman not under
femme in covert.

She beareth in a Lozenge as a maiden Lady B. a fess
wavey between 3 Goates heads erazed A. by ye name of
sedney, & is ye paternall Coate Armour of Mary sedney
sole daughter & heyre of Sr Charles sedney of Southfleet
in Kent Bart.

note if she be a widdow, then she Jmpaleth her paternall
Coate wth ye of her deceased husband in ye dexter part or side
note ye way for men to bear their wiues Coat if an ....
heiress is in an Escocheon of pretence wth is placed in ye
midst of ye shield, e if noe heiress then to be Jmpaled
wth their owne in ye sinister side.

possessing classes the times were quite clearly prosperous. The quarter-century of peace at home since the Restoration had seen great strides made in that accumulation of wealth which was the surest sign of success. Nowhere was this more obvious than in the City of London, now rebuilt in stone and brick after the Fire. London, an enormous city of half a million people, one-tenth of the whole population, was well on the way to eclipsing her great trading rival, Amsterdam. Here was concentrated the new plutocracy, whose fortunes had been made in that expansion of trade with the far corners of the world, which we have seen James encouraging at the Restoration. The ships massed in the river had brought in the exotic produce of every continent – tobacco from Virginia, sugar from the West Indies, colourful textiles from the Indian weavers of Coromandel, coffee, tea, spices and the rest of the spoil of the Orient. As the prices of such goods fell, a revolution in taste had taken place, as tobacco and tea came within the reach of ever poorer strata of the population, and a contemporary could write, 'the

145

English are not now so much addicted to gluttony and drunkenness, as of late years, but unto tobacco more'. In the next decade the *nouveaux riches* of the City were to buy political power with their wealth and become the back-bone of the Whigs, but in 1685 they had been tamed and made innocuous by changes brought about in the personnel of the City's government during the Tory reaction of Charles's last years.

For the moment, political power still rested where it had lain ever since the beginning of the century – in the Court and in the Country. Since the Restoration a whole new city had been built to the north and west of Whitehall, and it was in this fashionable West End that the courtiers and aristocrats, their mistresses and tradesmen lived, as far apart in behaviour and beliefs from the merchants to the east of them, as those merchants were from the sailors and stevedores who assured their continued wealth in the riverside hovels of the East End. However, to the men on whom the whole political system rested – the fifteen thousand gentlemen and squires of England who, as magistrates and landowners, ruled the countryside, and from whose numbers most of the five hundred Parliament men would be chosen – both Court and City were anathema. Macaulay, in his famous third chapter, has drawn a marvellously prejudiced picture of the English squire, 'a man with the deportment, the vocabulary, and the accent of a carter, yet punctilious on matters of genealogy and precedence, and ready to risk his life rather than see a stain cast on the honour of his house'. These ignorant, coarse and proud men were Tories born, and prized two things above all, hereditary monarchy and the Church of England, the two great supports of property and a suitably hierarchical society. But natural Tories as they were, they were capable of resistance to the Crown, once they were convinced that their security and liberty were in jeopardy, as they had proved in the early days of the Long Parliament and again during the Exclusion Crisis. It was these men who made their way up to Westminster in 1685 to deliberate on the support they were prepared to give to a Catholic king. The elections had been supervised by Sunderland, and 'such a landed parliament was never seen', the most reactionary and loyalist Parliament of the century, apparently cured of that Whiggish element so effectively managed by Shaftesbury only four years previously.

'Such a landed parliament was never seen'

146

While these very English gentlemen are cursing at the expense and the bare-faced swindling that they experience in the foreign land of London, let us look briefly at the situation in Europe in 1685. The attention of most people was on two great military machines, one moving slowly forward and the other slowly back. In the east the last great thrust of the Moslem Turks into the heart of Christendom had been foiled by the victory of the fat, heroic Polish King, John Sobieski, outside the walls of Vienna in 1683. By 1685 the victorious Christian army, in whose ranks were soldiers from almost every European nation, including England, had pushed the Turks right down the Great Hungarian Plain, and were soon to begin the siege of the great Turkish stronghold of Buda. But, bold as they were, many of the Christian soldiers were looking back over their shoulders to the west, where a man even more rapacious than the Sultan was poised to strike. For, ever since the Peace of Nijmegen in 1678, the soldiers of Louis XIV had been surreptitiously moving forward towards the Rhine. Strasbourg had been swallowed up in 1681, Luxembourg in 1684. Sooner or later the armies in the east would have to turn round and fight them, lest all of Europe become a French dominion. To no one was this clearer than Louis's great opponent, William of Orange.

From the day when William was appointed Stadholder and commander-in-chief of the forces of the United Provinces in 1672, to his death thirty years later, his policies were directed towards one aim – the destruction or containment of the French colossus. As a Protestant, as the owner of vast estates in his own right, and as the leader of the Dutch Republic, this stunted, unhealthy man was rightly alarmed at the ambitions and successes of France. In 1672 he had given the example of resistance himself, when he ordered the dykes to be opened and thus caused the advancing French army to be bogged down in the flooded fields of the Low Countries. Now in 1685, technically at peace, he was busily engaged in building up a grand alliance to be ready to destroy the French, when war should next break out. His most obvious ally in this venture was the great army of the Emperor Leopold, torn between success on the Danube and danger on the Rhine. But many other nations were afraid of France. To the south was Spain, once the bitterest opponent of the Protestant, republican Dutch and now their obvious ally against French aggression. To the east were Sweden, Denmark and the princes of the Empire who played their own power game against the background of general European mobilisation, now for France, now against her, for the most part more interested in their own expansion than in any such ethereal concept as the balance of power. And to the north-west lay the biggest question-mark of all, the three kingdoms of King James. Militarily insignificant in 1685 with only a small, though well-trained army, England was yet a potential arbiter in the European power struggle. Who could think back on the days of the Ironsides without respect for the English fighting-man, or forget the shattering effect of Blake's broadsides in the First Dutch War? For a generation an English king had shuffled between the French and the Dutch. What would his brother do? It was as much the answer to this question as the problem of his wife's inheritance that caused the half-Stuart, William of Orange, to keep his eye on England.

The Parliament of 1685 was a pointer to the future. Here was certainly no check to James's ambitions, whatever these might turn out to be. From the very first, James made clear to his Parliament of landed men that he expected them to be absolutely obedient. He wanted the revenues for life, and he would not allow any further need for money to be used as an excuse to present grievances to the Crown, as had been the practice of the hated institution in his father's and his brother's reigns. Such, he explained, 'would be a very improper method to take with me'. James's truculent attitude met little opposition in a House which had once prided itself on being the main safeguard of the liberties of landed men against the presumption of the Crown. James got the same revenues as Charles had received for life, and was soon to get more. Now that expanding trade had swelled the receipts of the customs, the main source of income, this would be more than sufficient to maintain his administration and his parsimonious style of life, as long as he avoided full-scale war. No other Stuart king ever received such bounty. Sunderland's management of the elections and James's repetition of his promise to defend the Church of England would have been sufficient to have ensured this in the current atmosphere of public opinion, but there was in fact something else in the wind which was to ensure Parliament's loyalty, and hence James's independence. For the last puff of the Whig fury, which had so nearly destroyed James in the Exclusion Crisis, was at that moment blowing two ill-fated and poorly organised expeditions towards their destruction. In the atmosphere of 1685 nothing could have better united the landed men behind the Crown than a Whig rebellion.

For James Scott, Duke of Monmouth, the sudden death of his father had been nothing short of disaster. As the figurehead of the left wing of the Exclusionists, the Protestant Duke could clearly expect little love from his uncle, nor was it likely that he would ever be able to return to England from his present place of exile in the Netherlands. Here, especially in the great trading city of Amsterdam, were worked out intrigues and plots as ingenious and normally futile as those engaged in by the Cavaliers in exile of James's youth. Republican and Calvinist Dutchmen had welcomed fleeing Englishmen ever since the Restoration, and were now, somewhat to William's embarrassment, the hosts of old Cromwellians, Anabaptists, Exclusionists and Whigs of every possible shade of political opinion. Monmouth found himself the focus of attention of one group of such plotters who, despite much evidence to the contrary, thought the time right for invasion of an England which they felt ready for rebellion against a Catholic king of known absolutist tendencies. The vain Monmouth did little to oppose the flattering intriguers, and soon was pawning his own, his mistress's and her mother's plate to pay for the chartering of a thirty-two gun frigate to carry his eighty or so supporters on their ill-fated voyage to Lyme Regis. Meanwhile another expedition with much more likelihood of success had already set off. The Duke of Argyll, whom James had so unwisely allowed to escape from prison four years earlier, sailed on 2 May with a strong body of Scots mercenary officers to raise his own clan, the Campbells, and the Covenanters in a rebellion planned to coincide with that of Monmouth. Once James's army, which the plotters rather optimistically expected to be riddled with disloyalty, had been split to deal with the two revolts, it was expected that Cheshire and London would also rise, and thus bring to a premature end the reign of Stuart despotism.

Nothing went right. The royal army in Scotland was forewarned of Argyll's expedition and prevented him from

James Scott, Duke of Monmouth, Charles II's favourite son. He had plotted with Shaftesbury and the Exclusionists during his father's lifetime, and therefore could expect little sympathy after his death. In 1685 he created an opposition Court at Amsterdam, and plotted his invasion of England. Portrait after Wissing.

capturing even his own stronghold of Inveraray. Once his supporters realised the power of the royal opposition, most of them deserted him, and those who remained were fatally divided on whether to concentrate on operating in the Covenanter lands of the south-west or in the Campbell country farther north. Argyll was captured and executed, and large numbers of his supporters were branded and transported for life to the West Indies. The Scottish government was rapidly passing out of the hands of the moderate Queensberry into those of James's friends, the Earls of Perth and Melfort, who were to be long remembered for their savage rule of the northern kingdom. The news of Argyll's defeat left Monmouth alone against his uncle, for neither Cheshire nor London had risen to support what were seen to be two singularly ill-managed and ill-timed revolts.

Monmouth's supporters had wisely chosen to land in the West Country which, except for Royalist Cornwall, was an area with a long tradition of left-wing politics and religion, where the Protestant Duke had been welcomed with great enthusiasm during his progress around the country in 1680. Initially, the rebellion had considerable success. The first line of defence, the county militia of Devon and Somerset, seemed reluctant to fight, and indeed many militia men deserted to Monmouth. They were joined by large numbers of West Countrymen, armed with everything from muskets, kept hidden since the Civil War, to scythes and bill-hooks. But such a rabble, although they might die well, were unlikely to offer much resistance to the royal army now moving towards the West Country, and Monmouth noted with growing apprehension the failure of the Whig gentry on whom he had counted to declare for him. By 1685, the gentlemen of Devon and Somerset were probably not as Whig as Monmouth, who had been out of the country for some time, thought, and in any case were for the most part unready to risk their whole fortune in support of a bastard claimant to the throne, many of whose entourage were declared republicans. So, as Monmouth made his way from Lyme to Taunton, where in front of enthusiastic crowds he was proclaimed King and proceeded to touch for the King's Evil, and then by stages to the crisis of his revolt before the walls of Bristol, metropolis of the west, he must have heard with growing fear of the approach of the royal army.

James's army, with only eight thousand men – minute by Continental standards – was still quite clearly too strong for Monmouth. Two of the regiments had just returned from brutal active service in Morocco, and most of the officers had seen action as mercenaries on the Continent. Monmouth, of course, as a former Captain-General of the forces, knew the army intimately, and many of its commanders were his personal friends. He had counted on a number of them deserting to him, but here again he had miscalculated. Three years later, many of them were to desert their King, but not in 1685. Monmouth's timing was all wrong. The commander-in-chief was, strangely enough, a Frenchman, Louis Duras, Earl of Feversham, a Protestant friend of James who had been in English service since 1660. He was the nephew of James's former master, Turenne, and though he had none of his uncle's genius he was, despite a reputation for gluttony and idleness, a perfectly competent soldier. His appointment had much annoyed the other obvious contestant for the post, John Churchill. Despite his sister's dismissal from the ducal bed, Churchill had remained in James's favour, as we have seen, and had also taken out some re-insurance through his wife's friendship with James's younger daughter, Princess Anne, who was now married to the ineffectual Prince George of Denmark. Churchill, who had already been assured of the command, was naturally aggrieved when the unpopular Frenchman was appointed over his head, and he was to continue to nurse the grudge in the future. But this potential division in the high command of the royal army was to do Monmouth little good.

As Monmouth marched in fairly good spirits towards Bristol, the royal army closed in. Lyme and Taunton had been retaken in his rear, and sections of the royal army under Churchill and the Moroccan veteran Kirke were on his flanks. But Monmouth's position was not yet hopeless. The royal army, still awaiting reinforcements, was not yet strong enough to risk battle and contented themselves with skirmishing and harassing the local population. Meanwhile Bristol, packed with dissidents of all types, weakly fortified and defended by a militia whose loyalty was extremely doubtful, lay before him. One bold throw might have given Monmouth the city; at least if he had fallen attacking such a distinguished place, he would have gone down with colours flying, but at the last minute he lost his nerve, and led his own dispirited and rapidly dwindling supporters back towards Bridgwater. Here, on the night of 5 July, he made one last brave effort. Realising that he still outnumbered the royal army commanded by Feversham, who were encamped on Sedgemoor outside the town, he determined to do the one thing that the regulars, confident that he was on the run, least expected. He resolved to attack the royal troops at night, and, had he been a little luckier, he might well have made up for the inexperience of his troops by the surprise of the move. But his cavalry under Lord Grey, a rakish crony of Monmouth with no experience of soldiering whatsoever, ran into a royal outpost and raised the alarm, while the whole of the rebel army found themselves non-plussed when they arrived at the Bussex Rhine, one of a number of wide ditches which lie across Sedgemoor. In fact they could have easily crossed it to attack the royal camp, where the soldiers, despite the alarm, were still half-asleep. But, in the darkness, it was impossible for non-locals to know how

The Declaration
of
James Duke of Monmouth

And of those noble men Gentlemen & Commons now in Arms for defence of the Protestant Religion, & Vindication of the Laws Rights & Priviledges of England from ye Invasion made upon them, & for delivering the Nation from ye Usurpation & Tyranny of James Duke of York

Forasmuch as it is apparent yt all Government is instituted onely to ye End yt people might under it find safty & Refuge from violence & oppression & not for ye private Interest or personall greatness of any man, It cannot be imagined yt mankind would part wth their naturall freedome & Liberty, & submitt themselves to government to ye End they might be more effectually destroyed by their Governors, than they could have been had they continued in ye State of Nature And such have been the transactions of affaires within this Nation for severall yeares last past, yt although ye Libertyes & Priviledges of ye people and ye Protestant Religion were fenced & hedged about by as many Lawes as ye wisdome of man could devise to preserve & defend them agt Popery & arbitrary power Our Lawes have been trampled under foot & ye libertyes & Priviledges thereby provided for violently ravished from us, And ye power intrusted wth ye Governors bent wholy to ye destruction of ye People Religion by Popish Councills undermined, wch was effected not onely by ye imoderate desire of ye Duke of York & those in power after an absolute Domination & Tyranny & ye Introduction of Popish Idolatry as subservient thereunto, But likewise from severall Innovations upon & changes of ye Ancient

Monmouth's declaration against James II, declaring him a usurper and a tyrant, and blaming him for all the disasters that had befallen the kingdom, including the death of Charles. The publication of this declaration sealed Monmouth's fate, for James would not consider his pleas for mercy thereafter.

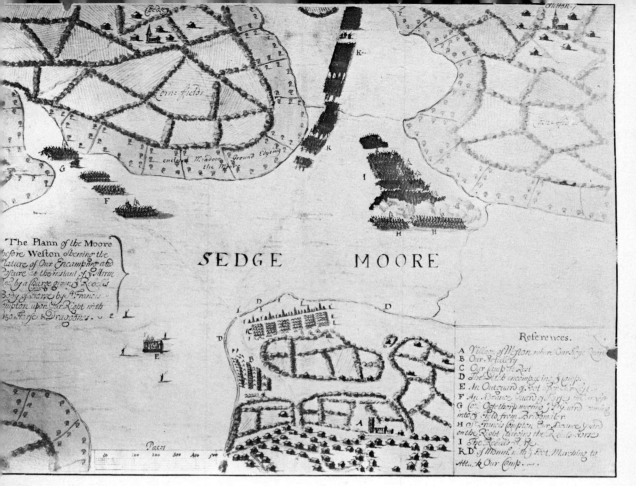

The Plann of the Moore before Weston shewing the Nature of Our Encamping and Posture at the instant of y^e Alarm by a Charge given y^e Rebells ... y^e distance by Sr Francis Compton upon Our Right with 150 Horse & Dragoons.

SEDGE MOORE

Corn: fields

enclosed Meadow & Ground adjoyning the River

References.

A Village of Weston where Our Army lay
B Our Artillery
C Our Camp at Rest
D The Ditch encamping ye Camp
E An Outguard of Foot upon ye Left
F An Advance Guard of Horse in ye way
G Col: Oglethorp meeting ye Army and coming into ye field from Br: Water
H Col: Francis Compton Our Horse ye yd on the Right charging the Rebells 1000
I The Rebells R.H.
K D of Monm: with ye Foot Marching to Attack Our Camp.

deep or wide it was, and the first light of dawn revealed the mass of West-Countrymen, armed with scythe and club, on the edge of the ditch, ready to be mowed down by the royal artillery or hacked to pieces by the cavalrymen. Monmouth, stripping off his armour, borrowed £100 from a faithful supporter and demonstrated that ability as a jockey which had so endeared him to the populace, by fleeing with Grey, leaving his foolish, faithful followers to their doom. A few days later, the elegant, swashbuckling Protestant Duke was dragged out of a fern-covered ditch in the New Forest by troopers of the Sussex Militia under Lord Lumley. The misery of the now ragged, starving Duke was not improved by a heavy cold, nor by the suggestion of the ever-cheerful Grey that 'if his cold was troubling him, King James had a ready cure for it'.

The total defeat of the two rebellions gave James the confidence he needed to move forward on policies close to his heart. But

ABOVE Plan of the Battle of Sedgemoor, which took place on 5 July 1685. The King's forces, under the command of Feversham, lie in the village of Weston at the bottom of the plan, protected by a ditch. At the top, Monmouth's infantry forces are approaching the royal camp and, to their left, the rebel cavalry is engaged with the King's, commanded by Sir Francis Compton.

RIGHT The Act of Attainder for high treason issued against Monmouth.

(7)

Anno Regni

Jacobi II. Regis.

An Act to Attaint *James* Duke of
Monmouth of High-Treason.

 Hereas James Duke of
Monmouth has in an
Hostile manner In-
vaded this Kingdom,
and is now in open
Rebellion, Levying
War against the
King, contrary to the Duty of his Al-
legiance; Be it Enacted by the Kings
B 2   most

(8)

most Excellent Majesty, by and with the
Advice and Consent of the Lords Spiritual and Temporal, and Commons in
this Parliament Assembled, and by the
Authority of the same, That the said
James Duke of Monmouth Stand and be
Convicted and Attainted of High-Treason, And that he suffer pains of Death,
and Incur all Forfeitures as a Traytor
Convicted and Attainted of High-Treason.

F I S.

first there was a small matter of reprisals, for James was not a merciful man. Monmouth, who two years earlier had managed to obtain a pardon from his father by implicating some of his friends in the Rye House Plot, tried the same trick again. Throwing himself at James's feet he begged for mercy. But he got short shrift from his royal uncle. Any hopes of mercy had disappeared with the publication of his declaration branding James as responsible for practically everything that had gone wrong in the kingdom, from the Fire of London to King Charles's death. A man like James did not take kindly to the accusation of fratricide, and on 15 July Monmouth was executed. This was a clumsy business in which the noted Ketch, to the fury of the sympathetic crowd, took five blows of his axe to do his work, and still had to finish off the job with a knife. 'Thus ended this quondam duke', wrote Evelyn, 'darling of his father and the ladies … debauch'd by lusts, seduc'd by crafty knaves. He failed and perished.' In the west the rebels caught in arms were to have an equally unpleasant time. Many received a summary execution at the hands of the notorious Colonel Kirke and his Moroccan veterans, ironically known as his Lambs. Those who survived were handed over to the judgment of the Bloody Assizes, the commission appointed to try captured rebels, presided over by Judge Jeffreys, an ambitious, bullying lawyer, who had made a successful career as the legal arm of James, since being appointed as his solicitor in 1677. Some three hundred of the rebels were hanged, drawn and quartered, their dismembered bodies being displayed all over the West Country as a warning to such a seditious area of the fruits of rebellion. A further thousand were transported, like Argyll's men, to the West Indies, many to die on the voyage. Some of their descendants still exist in Barbados as a community of poor whites, known locally as Redlegs. Lesser rebels were whipped near to death, and the whole of the West was punished by having royal regiments stationed in its midst. By the time of the General Pardon, issued on 10 March 1686, there was little opposition to the Crown left in the West Country, and Jeffreys might well feel that his pledge that 'Taunton and Bristol and the County of Somerset shall know their duty to God and their King before I leave them' had been fulfilled.

A subdued country and a subservient Parliament were the

Judge Jeffreys, James's notorious Chief Justice, who conducted the 'Bloody Assizes' to try Monmouth's supporters. Over three hundred were executed by hanging, drawing and quartering, and many hundreds more were transported and sold into slavery in the West Indies. On Jeffreys' return to London he was rewarded by James with the high office of Lord Chancellor. Portrait of *c.* 1678, painted by W. Claret.

background against which James prepared to inaugurate his Grand Design. Now he felt he could do anything without the fear of civil unrest, and Monmouth's rebellion thus acted as a catalyst, pushing James forward much faster than he might have gone had it not occurred, and thus, as we shall see, pushing him towards disaster. For the sort of England that James had it in mind to rule was not the sort of England that even a subdued country wished to be. James had a Grand Design which reflected in outline the plans of Coleman in the 1670s, but his view of an ideal nation embodied all of his experiences as a man. The soldier wanted a strong army on the French model; the sailor a powerful navy; and the English patriot wanted to see both of these independent of Continental financial control, and England the arbiter of European affairs. The trader and colonialist wanted to see the continued expansion of trade and empire protected by his powerful navy, trade bringing wealth to the mighty and work to the many, the Empire a microcosm of England and the mother-country's natural support. The recusant wanted to see complete liberty of conscience in England and her possessions overseas, for James, though devoted to his

156

own religion, was 'very positive in his opinion against all persecution for conscience sake' and felt that liberty of conscience would promote trade in England, as it appeared to have done in Holland. Finally, as a Stuart king, he wished to rule as a god, through ministers and bureaucracy of his own choice, without the impertinent advice of a Parliament, whose only function in his system was to approve his policies without discussion. To the twentieth-century mind, much of this programme seems eminently reasonable, and indeed it is James's methods, his lack of political sense and his poor choice of ministers, rather than his professed policy, which are most to be condemned. But to contemporaries, particularly those of the landed class, and thus his natural supporters, practically the whole programme was anathema. Even those policies which seemed least objectionable were seen as part of some devilish scheme on their monarch's behalf to lead the country to Rome. A standing army would be used to dragoon good Protestants into attendance at Mass; toleration was nothing but a subtle scheme to destroy the Church of England; independence abroad was but a sham. James, like his brother, would sell Protestant England to the King of France, and his navy would be used once more against the Dutch, now seen to be England's natural allies. Whether contemporary opinion was correct in its assessment of James's motives is pure conjecture, since he had no opportunity to complete his programme, but certainly the King did little to allay his countrymen's suspicions.

The most suspect aspect of James's behaviour was his own open Catholicism, and his constant encouragement of Catholics to take up positions of power. Only two days after his accession, he went publicly to Mass, and he continued to do so throughout his reign, even celebrating Mass before his abridged, but magnificent, Anglican coronation in Westminster Abbey. Many Catholics, often with considerable military experience as mercenaries on the Continent, had been commissioned in the army to assist in the suppression of Monmouth's rebellion, and James refused to dismiss them when the crisis was over, despite the continued existence of the Test Act. Both in Scotland and in Ireland, Catholic friends of James were coming to power, and the appointment of James's old friend Richard Talbot, Earl of Tyrconnel, as Lieutenant-General of the Irish army awoke old

157

The coronation procession of James II, showing the King walking under a canopy accompanied by his Gentlemen Pensioners. The procession is headed by the Duke of Somerset holding the orb, the Duke of Ormonde bearing the crown, and the Duke of Albemarle carrying the sceptre of the Dove. Samuel Pepys was one of the canopy-bearers at the coronation.

fears of invasion by Irish papist troops, which Tyrconnel, who had ambitions for Irish independence backed by French money, did nothing to allay. At Court, James's priests, and especially his English Jesuit confessor, Father Petre, who had been responsible for the upbringing of James's illegitimate children, did nothing to discourage the belief that toleration was anything other than a sham to allow the Jesuit conquest of the country. And as soon as they realised that to be Catholic promised jobs and profitable pickings, first a trickle and then a swarm of Catholic lords and gentlemen descended on Whitehall. Not to be outdone, many non-Catholics of easy conscience, conspicuous amongst them the adaptable Sunderland, joined their royal master in his public celebrations of Mass.

James's promotion of Catholics, though understandable, did him no good in a country where many still believed in the reality of the Popish Plot, and the ostentatious refusal of many Anglican courtiers, such as Rochester, to follow their king into his chapel was a sign of the resistance that a pro-Catholic policy was likely to engender. James's attempts to convert his fellow-subjects had little success, even among those whose faith was not their most conspicuous characteristic. Despite his habit of taking men aside and earnestly discussing religion with them, often emphasising the points of his argument by referring to

RIGHT Warrant of 12 June 1685 signed by James II's Queen, Mary of Modena, to the warden commissioners and comptroller of the Mint, directing them to prepare her Great Seal, with detailed drawings of the obverse and reverse.

some papers left behind by Charles, explaining the reasons for his last minute conversion, only a few people, such as the Drummond brothers and later Sunderland, apostasised. Some men threw James off with a jest, like the cynical Kirke who said 'that he was already pre-engaged, for he had promised the King of Morocco, that if ever he changed his religion, he would turn Mahometan'. But others, more devout, were irritated and upset

An embassy from the Pope to James II, disembarking at the river stairs of Old Somerset House.

by James's proselytising, and suspicious of what might follow the failure of private argument to convert them. This general atmosphere of suspicion was much strengthened by contemporary events in France, a country which James was rightly suspected of admiring. For, on 17 October 1685, Louis XIV revoked the eighty-seven-year-old Edict of Nantes, the main protection of his Protestant subjects, and a flood of Huguenot refugees left France for more congenial homes. The timing was bad luck for James, and, though he professed abhorrence of Louis's intolerance, and welcomed the refugees, this did not quiet the fears of his own Protestant subjects, who learned with horror of the methods used by Louis to try to convert his heretical countrymen. One Catholic king was likely to be much the same as another.

It was in such an atmosphere of public alarm that James recalled Parliament in November 1685. He did nothing to dispel such alarm. Using as an excuse the failure of the West Country militia to do much to check Monmouth, he demanded extra funds to strengthen the royal army. This in itself was enough to frighten the members of the House of Commons who heard

160

his demands. For it was just such Tory gentlemen who commanded the militia, and they looked on the institution, rude as it was, as their main protection against royal despotism. Many may have agreed with Dryden's description of the poorly-trained yokels who filled its ranks, as 'mouths without hands, maintained at vast expense; in peace a charge, in war a weak defence'. But they were infinitely preferable to a large standing army under the ultimate command of the King. Ever since Cromwell, the army had been hated, and there were few men in the House who had not heard of a more contemporary example of military despotism. For King Louis's agents of conversion had been his dragoons. The Essex gentleman Sir John Bramston echoed the feelings of the House in his autobiography: 'The rebellion being quelled, and their general headless, the danger was over, and so no cause to continue the men any longer in arms.' But James was insistent, not only in his demand for money to strengthen the army, but also, far worse, in his determination to retain his Catholic officers in their commissions. It was on this point that a subdued grumbling in the House became a distinct opposition to the Crown. James was furious. Eleven days after Parliament had been recalled, it was prorogued, never to meet again. Later in his reign James was to try to find a Parliament even more loyal than this one had appeared to be, but it was a difficult task. As Bishop Burnet remarked, 'in all England it would not have been easy to have found five hundred men, so weak, so poor, and so devoted to the Crown, as these were'. So far had James alienated the natural support of the Crown, the most Cavalier Parliament of the century, in just over six months of his reign.

But by the end of 1685 James had hardly even started to establish his Grand Design. There was much to do, but, with the revenues already voted for life, he did not need Parliament's help to do it. James spent most of the following year, 1686, in strengthening his position, and removing from his councils those people who seemed determined to thwart him. By the end of the year most of the moderates and convinced Anglicans had been replaced. Halifax and the Hydes had gone, and the ever-scheming Sunderland was firmly in control, hinting at the possibility of his conversion, anticipating his master's every wish, courting James's priests and his Queen, but, like a wise gambler, hedging against the prospects of disaster by accepting a large pension from Louis xiv on the one hand, and encouraging his wife's friendships with the great Whig ladies and the Dutch on the other. Other appointments confirmed the trend of the times. Jeffreys became Lord Chancellor, and four Catholic lords were appointed to the Privy Council. Meanwhile, in Scotland, the Drummond brothers, and, in Ireland, Tyrconnel, consolidated their positions.

James and Sunderland began to set the scene for the further bombshells they had in mind for 1687. In March the King issued his general pardon, releasing from the prison not only the survivors of Monmouth's rebellion, but also a flock of dissenters who had been prosecuted under the penal laws. Already James was thinking that support from the left wing of religion might be valuable, if he wished to introduce his policy of toleration, and in this he was much encouraged by the friendship of the Quaker Penn, son of the Commonwealth admiral who had been James's right-hand man in the Battle of Lowestoft. In June a collusive court case rather tardily approved James's prerogative rights to suspend the penal laws and Test Acts in particular cases. Even more Catholic officers received commissions, and that summer James's rapidly expanding army camped on Hounslow Heath, its drill and mock battles a reminder to the nearby City of London of its master's military strength, the Mass said openly in the tents of his religion. In July the first move was made in a long offensive against the Anglican Church, the traditionally aquiescent supporter of the Crown, which James had sworn so manfully to defend. An Ecclesiastical Commission was set up to exercise jurisdiction over the Church. Headed by Jeffreys, and including among its members that well-known churchman, the Earl of Sunderland, it was empowered to suspend or deprive of his living any clergyman of the Established Church. One of its first victims was Henry Compton, a Whig aristocrat and former soldier, now Bishop of London, whose offence had been to refuse to suspend one of his clergy who had preached against the Catholic religion. Compton was to be a dangerous enemy, the man who more than anyone else roused the Church from its accustomed lethargy, and forced its ten thousand or so clergymen to interrupt their games of bowls and shovelboard in order to consider whether devotion to their Church might not override devotion to their King. But, for the moment, they remained quiet, and confined themselves to muttering among themselves and to their natural allies in the countryside, the Tory gentry.

By 1687, James was ready to move a little faster. Deaf to the muttering in the countryside, impressed by the lack of any real resistance to his policies, and encouraged by the gratitude of the released Quakers and other dissenters, he issued at the beginning of the year a royal proclamation suspending practically all the penal laws against religion. In April this was followed by a declaration of liberty of conscience which released his non-Anglican subjects from obeying the Test Acts. Everyone was now allowed to practise his own religion, without incurring any penalty, and offices were open to people of any religion, though, since so many offices were ultimately the gift of the King, it paid to be a Catholic. This was, of course, the catch. Toleration is an attractive policy, and James was flooded with petitions expressing the gratitude of his dissenting and Catholic subjects, but the least astute had no difficulty in observing that, in a world unrestricted by penal laws against religion, it was Catholics who got the best jobs, and to the more suspicious there was little doubt that toleration was but the spearhead for Jesuit domination of the country.

One strange thing about James's behaviour as king is that although he insisted constantly on his right to use his prerogative powers, and particularly the power to dispense with existing legislation, he was also determined that the major institutions in the kingdom should be seen to support his policies. He was especially keen to have the repeal of the penal laws and the Test Act approved by Parliament. His main motive in this was that he thought that only thus could he insure the continuation of his policies by his successors on the throne. Long before his declarations of toleration in 1687, he had tried to browbeat the members of Parliament into pledging their support for repeal. This 'telling of noses', as Bramston put it, was very awkward for the members, who were forced to enter the royal closet and either agree to a policy of which they disapproved or be disgraced. Most hedged, saying they would wait until they heard the debates in Parliament, or else, like Bramston, avoided running into the King. Seeing that he was getting nowhere,

163

James eventually dissolved his Parliament in July 1687, and was to spend the rest of his reign in an unsuccessful attempt to rig the elections sufficiently to find a more compliant one.

The lengths to which he and Sunderland were prepared to go in this policy were fantastic. A circular was sent to all lords lieutenant of the counties, ordering them to summon the prominent men, and to ask them three specific questions concerning their opinions about the repeal of the penal laws and Test Acts, and their general attitude towards toleration, in an attempt to find sufficient men to support the King's policies in the next Parliament. The response to this early example of an opinion poll was very disappointing. It had the effect of forcing the country to consider where they stood in relation to James's policies, and the collusive nature of many of the replies shows that the matter was much discussed in the countryside. For seventeenth-century man, as now, discussion was the god-mother to resistance, and James would have done well not to encourage it. From the replies that still exist, it can be seen that nearly a third of the persons polled gave an outright refusal to support the King's policy in Parliament, and another quarter refused to commit themselves, an attitude which was tantamount to opposition. A lead to the gentry was often given by the lords lieutenant themselves, and such outspoken opponents of toleration found themselves quickly dismissed from office, to be replaced often by Roman Catholics, or by those totally committed to James's policies, such as Sunderland and Jeffreys. But even this made little difference, and the general attitude is summed up by the Duke of Norfolk, who wrote directly to the King, that, from the three counties for which he was responsible, 'he could have brought all those in favour of repeal up with him in his coach, without the least harm to his horses'.

Having failed to find support among the Anglican gentry, James made an extraordinary *volte-face* for a prince whose whole youth had been dominated by the execution of his father and his exile in France. He turned for support to those he had often branded as fanatics and republicans in the past, the dissenters. His new lords lieutenant and other agents were instructed to seek them out in the countryside and in the towns, whose charters, which had recently been revised by Charles to exclude just such exclusionist and Whig people from the franchise, were now revised again by his brother to put them back. Such an extraordinary alliance of Catholic and dissenter, despite their common interest in toleration, must always rest on an insecure basis. For dissenters were normally far more anti-papist than the Anglicans. Few men could forget the memory of such events as the storming of Bolton, one of the bloodiest episodes in the Civil War, when Catholic Cavaliers had hacked to pieces the Puritan townsfolk of the 'Geneva of the North'. But James was impressed by the gratitude with which the dissenters had received his Declaration of Indulgence, and he was also impressed with the fighting spirit of the Puritans. It was this spirit, which James had seen in victory at the Battle of the Dunes and had heard about in defeat at Sedgemoor, that he hoped to enlist in his cause. James's efforts to turn the whole of English politics upside down, and create a counterweight to the solid body of Anglican opposition to his policies, by effecting a combination of Catholics and dissenters, culminated in the appointment to the Privy Council in July 1688 of the son of Sir Harry Vane, the fanatical Fifth Monarchy Man and re-publican who had been executed for high treason in 1662. In the new order, Vane made a suitable bedfellow to the Jesuit Father Petre, a member of the Council since the previous June, but neither they, nor Sunderland, nor indeed James himself, could disguise the fact that the mass of the country, even though they remained quiet, were solidly against them.

Fear of civil war and of James's army was the main reason for the strangely apathetic behaviour of his subjects, as he rode down their laws, their religion and their privileges. But there was another important factor encouraging an attitude of non-resistance. James was getting old for a seventeenth-century man, and people were confident that his Protestant successors, his daughter Mary and her husband William, would reverse his policies. It seemed better to wait out the bad times than to risk life and fortune against James's royal troops. The fact of James's age and his lack of a Catholic heir worried the Catholic party as much as it gave confidence to their opponents. James himself tried in vain to convert both his daughters, bombarding them with letters explaining the errors of Anglicanism, and sup-porting his attack by flourishing at them those papers of his brother's in which he had announced his conviction of the

Heemskerck's painting of
the Oxford election of
1688 in the Guildhall.
At the back is James II's
messenger, ordering the
election of his nominee
for alderman.

rightness of the Roman religion. But to no avail; Mary,
supported by William, and Anne by Lady Churchill, were deaf
to their father's appeals. Thwarted, the extreme Catholics
thought of a new idea, inspired no doubt by memories of
Shaftesbury and Monmouth. Mary would be excluded from
the succession, and the Duke of Berwick, James's eldest son by
Arabella Churchill, made the heir to the throne. But James,
the legitimist, would have none of this. His solution was more
naïve, but as it turned out more effective. In September 1687,
during a tour to rally support in the West, he rode out to the
miraculous well of St Winefrede and prayed for a son. Within
a fortnight Mary of Modena was pregnant, a fact which had
percolated through the consciousness of the nation by the end
of the year. The Catholic party was triumphant; they knew
it would be a boy. How did they know, whispered a suspicious
nation, aware of the fact that the Queen had gone five years
without a pregnancy, and was generally supposed to be in-

capable of bearing any more children. For the first six months of 1688, the great talking-point in England, and indeed in many parts of Europe, was the Queen's 'Great Belly ... of which people have different sorts of jealousies'.

James was jubilant. He seems never to have considered the possibility of a girl, or the fact that of Mary's six previous pregnancies, two had resulted in miscarriages, three children had died in their first year and the fourth at the age of four. The Queen's belly was the sign that God approved his policy, and all caution went to the wind. A confident James and his ever-energetic minister Sunderland, now ready to declare his conversion to Rome as a counter to the growing trust being placed in Father Petre, prepared to bully the Church of England into submission. But they had already gone too far. Great was their surprise when the attempt to impose a Catholic President on Magdalen College led to defiance by the Fellows, and a scandalous uproar in that training-ground of Anglican clergy-men, the University of Oxford. The attempt was successful, and Magdalen College became a thinly disguised seminary for Catholic priests, but James had managed to alienate yet another of the traditional supports of the Crown. The Royalist Uni-versity of Oxford, where James had spent most of the Civil War, was now to join in the ranks of resistance to the Crown. But the scandal at Oxford was nothing to what happened a few weeks later, on 27 April 1688, when an order was made to the Anglican clergy throughout the kingdom to read James's Declaration of Indulgence from the pulpit on four successive Sundays. The pulpit was the seventeenth century's main instrument in instructing the masses, and such a royal order was a king's quickest way of indicating his wishes to his people. But to ask the Anglican clergy to read a declaration which effectively removed their own privileges was really going a little too far. Inspired by the suspended Bishop Compton and other stalwarts, a large number of the clergy had decided that there was no future in the policy of non-resistance. Just before the date on which the first reading was supposed to take place, a party of seven bishops, including Archbishop Sancroft, crossed the river from Lambeth to Whitehall, and presented to the King a peti-tion in which they stated their refusal to read the Declaration. The seven bishops were the figure-heads of clerical resistance on a nationwide scale, and the King was correspondingly furious. Disregarding the advice of both Sunderland and Jeffreys to let the bishops off with a warning to behave in the future, he decided to have them arrested on a charge of seditious libel, and a few days later they were sent to the Tower.

Copies of the bishops' petition were published by well-wishers, and provided thoughtful reading for a London surprised and suspicious at the news that the Queen had gone into labour at St James's Palace some weeks earlier than had been expected. Public opinion was certain that a changeling Prince of Wales was about to be foisted on the nation. Mary of Modena had done little to dispel suspicions. Unusually prudish, she had refused to allow anyone to see her belly or feel the baby during her pregnancy, not even her jealous and inquisitive step-daughter Anne, who told her husband, Prince George of Denmark, that 'she had sometimes staid by her even indecently long in mornings to see her rise, and to give her her shift; but she never did either'. Prudish as Mary might be, she was unable to avoid the customary royal indignity of giving birth before a large number of witnesses. Over thirty people crowded into the small room at St James's Palace on a hot June morning to listen to the Italian Queen cry out in agony in her labour pains. She would have had to have been a consummate actress to have fooled all of them, even though the witnesses included a disproportionate number of Catholic supporters of James's policies. Burnet's story of the warming-pan which was slipped into her bed, but not opened 'that it might be seen that there was fire and nothing else in it', though providing entertaining matter for conjecture, clearly has no significance. Mary gave birth to a baby all right. The real problem is that, on account of the heat and stuffiness of the room, the midwives and Lady Sunderland took the baby into an adjoining chamber, before the child had been shown to the assembled multitude. Was the baby a girl, to be replaced by a healthy, male changeling – the miller's son of fable? There is room for doubt, but all the same it is clear that what evidence exists is overwhelmingly in support of the fact that James Francis Edward Stuart, to be known to another generation as the Old Pretender, was the son of James II and Mary of Modena, and thus the rightful heir to the throne of England. But, since there was room for doubt,

OPPOSITE The seven bishops who dared to defy James's order that the Declaration of Indulgence should be read in every Anglican pulpit on four successive Sundays. This action made them national figureheads of clerical resistance against the King's government. *Top row:* Francis Turner, Bishop of Ely; William Lloyd, Bishop of St Asaph; *Middle Row:* Thomas Ken, Bishop of Bath and Wells; William Sancroft, Archbishop of Canterbury; John Lake, Bishop of Chichester; *Bottom row:* Jonathan Trelawney, Bishop of Bristol; Thomas White, Bishop of Peterborough. English glass picture of *c.* 1688.

The huge bed made for James in 1687 by Thomas Roberts, the King's cabinet maker. It now stands in the Venetian Ambassador's Room at Knole Park, Kent, and still retains its rich carving and gilding and hangings of green velvet. It was probably the bed in which Mary of Modena gave birth to the Old Pretender.

it was foolish of James to order an enquiry into the birth to remove the stain on his wife's honour. The enquiry proved nothing conclusively, and merely gave strength to the suspicion that there was something extremely fishy about the whole business. And in the current mood of public opinion, now seriously alarmed that James's pro-Catholic policies might become a permanent fixture under a Catholic heir, it was tactless, to say the least, to celebrate his triumph by inviting the Pope to be the child's godfather.

But James was certain now that he could not lose. Nineteen days after the birth of the Prince of Wales, the trial of the seven bishops began. Rarely can Anglican bishops have been so popular. An enormous crowd surrounded Westminster Hall, shouting their approval of the bishops' defiance of the King and their opinion of the paternity of the Prince of Wales. Even

Italian engraving
commemorating the birth
of James Francis Stuart,
the Old Pretender, on
20 June 1688.

James was alarmed, especially when he discovered that the feelings of the London mob were shared by many of the soldiers in his great camp at Hounslow. Just under three years after Sedgemoor the spirit of non-resistance to the royal will was disappearing. The change was echoed in the court room. In the atmosphere of hostility within the court the judges lost their nerve, or remembered their law, and two out of four summed up quite clearly in the bishops' favour. It was enough. Despite pressure put on the jury, who were kept up all night without light or water, the defendants were found 'not guilty', and the seven bishops were acquitted. The crowd went wild, cheering and mobbing the bishops as they left the court and, once again, their cheers were echoed in the camp at Hounslow. The sands had run out for James II, though even now he did not realise it.

171

7
The
Protestant
Wind
1688-9

A. Schoonebeek del. et fec.

CROWDS CAN CHEER, bishops can resist, a whole nation can be disaffected and despondent; but such emotions are a long way from rebellion. England in the summer of 1688 was still for the most part the cowed England which remembered with fear and horror the rotting quarters of the Mendip miners and ploughboys who had been so unwise as to rise against their King. What could men do? By the time of the trial of the seven bishops, James had succeeded in alienating nearly the whole of the ruling class in his kingdom. The Tory gentry and the Anglican clergy had long been disillusioned of their belief in James's promises at his accession; all that now remained was innate loyalty to an anointed king. But disillusion had gone much further; the very people whom James's policies seemed most to favour joined in the public joy at the acquittal of the bishops. All except the extreme Catholics found themselves terrified at the speed with which the Jesuit-inspired James was moving. They had too much experience of England to expect anything but a Protestant reaction, and even while they continued to draw their salaries from their unexpected promotions, hoped vainly that the King might soon do something to alleviate the public hatred that was rising up against them, or else made plans for flight in the event of disaster. The dissenters, too, were disillusioned, convinced by the propaganda of Halifax and others that toleration was but a snare to win their support for a monarch who would jettison them as soon as he was sure of success. But, even if universal disaffection was expressed in English homes, few Englishmen were prepared to fight against their king. For James II was no Charles I, waiting beside his royal standard at Nottingham for loyal men to join him. James was now the master of an army five times the size of the force which had defeated Monmouth, quite big enough to keep his critical subjects quiet. Or was it? The Protestant cheers from the army camp on Hounslow Heath were a happy omen for a people whom Evelyn describes as 'praying incessantly for an east wind' to deliver them from popish tyranny.

The east wind was the Protestant wind of 'Lilliburlero', the song of the moment, the wind that kept papists in Ireland, but would fill the sails of a Dutch invasion. To pray for such a wind was a strange prayer for a people who once had cheered a sailor-duke; but the only prayer left. What else but foreign

ABOVE Pewter relief of James II, dressed in Roman armour and wearing a laurel wreath, and dated 888 for 1688. It was almost certainly prepared for a medal, but never used because of the King's abrupt departure.

PREVIOUS PAGES Dutch engraving representing Britannia welcoming William and Mary to England on 5 November 1688, while James flees the country.

174

troops could now upset a papist prince with a powerful army? And who else could lead those troops in their crusade, but the Prince of Orange, that Protestant half-Stuart with a dutiful Stuart wife? Unpleasant though it was, it seemed the only solution, but one which a generation of constitutional lawyers and uneasy clerics were to find difficult to justify. The chronicles of England and the Old Testament were to be ransacked to search for precedent. William was to be the new David raised up by God to avenge Him and save His Church; the new Henry VII, the conqueror who won his crown in trial by battle. But, for the moment, he was just the Prince of Orange, an ambitious man much troubled by piles, a nasty cough and the problem of co-ordinating the activities of half Europe to ensure the successful deposition of his uncle.

How long had William had ambitions for the Crown of the three kingdoms? He certainly had a passion for sovereignty. The worst thing that Louis ever did to him was to seize the tiny enclave of Orange in south-east France which gave him his name and made him a prince. Some writers have suggested that William had always wanted to be King of England. The only Protestant male in the immediate succession, he had reinforced his claim by marrying his cousin Mary, the Protestant elder daughter of his papist uncle. For years he had played out his cautious hand, building up for himself a reputation and a promise as a possible Protestant saviour of the nation. During the Exclusion Crisis he had held himself ready to intervene, but the time was not yet ripe. Later, in Monmouth's rebellion, he had put the knife into his popular rival. He did nothing to prevent the planning and organisation of the rebellion in the Netherlands, but, once the expedition had sailed, he sent the six Anglo-Scots regiments permanently established in the Low Countries to help his uncle put down the revolt. As it turned out, they were not needed, but William won both ways; a dutiful nephew, but one whose main rival in the eyes of Protestant and Whiggish Englishmen was to perish on the block. In 1688 the English had no one else to turn to, and William was ready to accept their invitation. The fact that such an invitation entirely suited his foreign policy as Stadholder of the United Provinces was of course a very considerable bonus. For, as we have seen, William was entirely committed to the

destruction of Louis XIV, and one of the most jealously guarded prerogatives of an English king was the right to determine foreign policy and declare war. The Catholic James could never be trusted, or indeed expected, to wage war against France, his natural support in his popish policies. There was only one man whom William entirely trusted to do that – himself.

So, whether as an ambitious Stuart, a Protestant or an enemy of France, William had every reason to wish to be King of England. But the wish would not be an easy one to fulfil. Invasion of England was notoriously difficult, and James was rapidly building up his army and navy. If William were to get pinned down on English soil, not only his own life, but all that he had ever stood for would be in jeopardy. For, the moment that he was out of the way with a large number of troops, he could expect a French army to march into the Netherlands to do the job they had failed to do in 1672. And, once he was gone and the Netherlands were under French control, who then could stop Louis XIV from extending his conquests to the rest of Europe? Success in England therefore rested on a number of very important pre-requisites, as well as the normal quota of luck on which every successful man must count. England itself must be so disaffected that there would be virtually no opposition to his show of force. France must be engaged elsewhere than on the borders of the Netherlands, and these borders must in any case be guarded by a second army. This in turn would necessitate a treaty with another military potentate who might be interested in the containment of France. Finally, he must be able to trust the Dutch themselves, for the ruling merchant class, with their large market in France, had never felt so hostile to Louis as did William. By November 1688 all these conditions had been met, the east wind blew, and William was successful. It was a remarkable achievement, and William is certainly a remarkable man, if also a lucky one. But God, as is well known, is always on the side of successful Calvinists.

Much of William's success lay in the excellence of his propaganda and his intelligence service, which was second only to that of Louis XIV in size, and much better in its assessment of English information. A stream of remarkably accurate news flowed back to William in the Netherlands from his spies, the

OPPOSITE William III on horseback riding along the shore, over emblems of war, observed by Neptune and greeted by Ceres and Flora with the attributes of Peace and Plenty. This portrait of William was painted by Godfrey Kneller in 1700.

ABOVE Mary of Modena, James's second wife: portrait by Godfrey Kneller.

RIGHT James II, painted by Godfrey Kneller. This portrait was probably painted in the year of James's accession to the throne.

most successful of whom were often disaffected Scotsmen. While William wrote polite and non-committal letters to his uncle, he was learning all the time of the unease felt by many sections of the English population at James's apparently pro-papist policies. A more positive indication of this unease was the number of people who either came over to swell the already large number of English and Scottish refugees in the Nether-lands, or else opened rather guarded correpondence with William himself. Henry Sidney, uncle of the Earl of Sunderland, former ambassador to The Hague and a close friend of William's, was quite often to be seen in William's Court. Long committed to the Orangist cause, he was to play a vital role in the necessary liaison between Holland and England. Danby, Charles's minister who had been released from prison early in James's reign, was the key man in England. He it was, before his fall, who had negotiated William's marriage with Mary, and now he did not shrink from the logic of his policies in the 1670s. He still retained that knowledge of English opinion which had been so valuable as a manager of Parliament, and now he could use that knowledge and his local power in Yorkshire to effect the deliverance of his beloved Anglican religion. From early on, he was one of William's most distinguished English corres-pondents.

Assured of the support of Sidney, Danby and many others, William could feel that things were moving along quite nicely, and soon it was time to send off a more distinguished personal agent. The amiable, smooth Everard van Weede, Lord of Dijkvelt, had a double mission. He was to negotiate with James on the subject of what he intended to do with the large forces he was building up, but he was also to see as many of James's most influential subjects as he could. To them he was to paint an attractive picture of his master, as a fairly liberal Prince who, though he did not believe in the wisdom of the repeal of the Test Acts, approved in very general terms of religious toleration. In other words, William, if he came to the throne, would support the Anglican establishment, but, as a Calvinist himself, he would expect toleration for dissenters. Dijkvelt did his job well, and returned home in the summer of 1687 with a post-bag full of letters from distinguished Englishmen, including both James's brothers-in-law, one of his best soldiers and closest

friends, Lord Churchill, former ministers such as Danby and Halifax, and other men who as leaders of local opinion expressed views widely held in the English countryside and could back them up by raising their tenantry and other local forces. All these letters were naturally guarded, but they all tended to imply that in the last resort the writers would look to William to protect the Protestant religion in England.

Such contacts, once established, could easily be maintained and even extended. Further special envoys were to follow Dijkvelt and the network of spies continued its activities, while William was engaged in building up his army and navy, and negotiating with the other powers of Europe. As the hopes for Protestantism deteriorated in England, so did the stream of refugees to the Netherlands increase, and the wording of letters become less guarded. The Queen's pregnancy, the birth of the Prince of Wales and the imprisonment of the seven bishops all helped to build up the tension, and to push people towards a position from which there was no retreat. Eventually William got what he wanted – a direct invitation from seven leading Englishmen to invade England. He was assured that many of the English soldiers would desert because of their 'aversion to the popish religion' and that 'amongst the seamen it is almost certain that there is not one in ten who would do them any service in such a war'. The signatories included the Whigs Henry Sidney and Henry Compton, Bishop of London, and the Tory Earl of Danby, landed magnates and exclusionists. In so far as seven people can represent a cross-section of the ruling class they did so. And of course the seven men who were prepared to commit themselves like this were only the tip of the iceberg. William's spies had assured him that if things went only moderately well, many more great men would come over to his side, and that, as in most times of trouble, 'the number of those who desired to sit still' would be the greatest of all. A flood of propaganda poured off the Dutch printing-presses assuring the English people of William's desirable qualities and his intention of protecting the Protestant religion against the papist onslaught. A well-organised network of spies and well-wishers quickly distributed the pamphlets to an expectant population.

Meanwhile matters in Europe, ably assisted by William's diplomacy, had been going very well. William had protected himself by making an alliance with Brandenburg, and the Elector had sent troops to defend the Dutch borders against French aggression. In the Netherlands, too, he had been successful. Supported by his friend Fagel, the Grand Pensionary, he had persuaded the merchant oligarchy to back his policies. In this he had been helped considerably by a French tariff war against Holland which had done much to undermine the traditional friendship of Dutch merchants for their French customers. Far away in the east, the siege of Buda had been successfully completed, to be followed by the great victory of Mohacs in August 1687, and the Austrians and their allies, including Prince George of Hanover, later George I, were busy extending their conquests over the rest of Hungary. Soon, it was felt, they would be ready to turn round and face the French threat in the west. Louis, aware of this, was pressing forward with his diplomatic and military preparations for a massive invasion of the Palatinate on the Middle Rhine. The big question in William's mind was whether Louis was also preparing, either to attack the Netherlands, or to send an army across to England to help James. Louis certainly had both these courses of action in mind. One great army was poised to strike at William and yet another was offered to James. Would all the preparations be for nothing? William was in a terrible state of anxiety: 'My sufferings, my disquiet, are dreadful.' But

'My sufferings, my disquiet, are dreadful'

James refused the offer of French assistance, fearful of the effect this might have on English opinion; and, in the end, Louis very seriously underestimated the genius of William. Feeling William's invasion plans had no hope at that time of year, he sent all four of his armies into the Palatinate in late September, including the one that was threatening the Dutch border. By doing so, Louis did much to ensure that his first cousin James lost his throne.

What had James been doing all this time? We have seen that part of his policy as king had been to recover that independence in foreign policy which his brother had lost by the secret clauses in the Treaty of Dover. No one could blackmail James for being a papist, since the whole world knew it. However, James's independence turned out to be a weakness rather than a strength. While Europe armed and took sides in the contest that all knew must come, James dithered. The result was that both France and the Netherlands were suspicious of what he intended to do with the military and naval forces he was building up. William was particularly worried that he intended to repeat the Anglo-French aggression of 1672 with another combined naval and military attack. Such a worry was much increased in the first weeks of 1688 by a request from James that the Anglo-Scots regiments in the Netherlands be repatriated. These men, whom, as we have seen, William sent over to help in the suppression of the Monmouth rebellion, were four thousand of the best troops in Europe. Despite their nationality, they considered their first loyalty to be to the Prince of Orange, and William, after some delay, refused to send them to James. James was furious; but all he got for his efforts were a few individual officers who resigned their commissions and came back to England. They were rapidly replaced by William with seasoned mercenaries or military refugees, and these six Anglo-Scots regiments were to be the spearhead of his invasion force. As for James, when the invasion came, he was to have virtually no foreign support. He had rejected the offer of French assistance, and nearly the whole of the rest of Europe was combining against France. Even the Pope, the man most reviled by popular Protestant fury in England, was against France, and thus would do nothing to disturb William's plans for the invasion of England. James had to rely on his own army and navy, but

unfortunately the report sent to William on the potential loyalty of the English troops was only too accurate.

By September 1688, James and his minister Sunderland were just about the only people in Europe who did not seem to believe that the ships massing in the Dutch ports and the troops marching in from all over the United Provinces, and from as far away as Sweden and Brandenburg, were intended for an invasion of England. James's intelligence in the Netherlands and at home was very poor, and his instincts as a sailor told him that no one would try to invade England in the late autumn. He felt certain that the army was to be used against France, and did not realise till the middle of the month what was obvious to thousands of his subjects. When the truth dawned, both James and Sunderland panicked. Urged on by a now terrified and broken Sunderland, James's initial reaction to the realisation of invasion was to try to curry favour in the country by reversing his previous policies. Lords lieutenant and magistrates were restored, and their dissenter and Catholic replacements dismissed; the bishops were courted, and the offer of a free election for a Parliament was made. It is possible that if James had summoned Parliament he could have saved himself, even at this late hour, though he would have had to make many concessions. But he was really far too late, and, after the first period of panic, his resolution returned. He would not throw all his policies away for an invasion scare. He dismissed the wavering and now useless Sunderland, who had spent the previous weeks frantically searching for somewhere to fly. Louis did not want him, but eventually through his wife's connections with the Dutch he was able to flee to Rotterdam.

Meanwhile James was determined that there would be no more concessions and prepared to defend himself. The military man took over. The unpopular Roman Catholic Admiral Sir Roger Strickland, who had nearly caused a mutiny by his insistence on saying Mass on board ship, was replaced as commander of the fleet by James's loyal friend the Protestant George Legge, Lord Dartmouth. Dartmouth was instructed to concentrate his fleet on the east coast in readiness for the expected Dutch attack. Lord Churchill, another of James's oldest friends, a Protestant like Dartmouth, was appointed Lieutenant-General and second-in-command of the army, but

OPPOSITE John Churchill, James's second-in-command against the invasion of William in 1688. Twenty years before, John had acquired a post in James's household through the influence of his sister, Arabella, but he now deserted to William, with his wife Sarah and her close friend, James's own daughter, Anne. This portrait, by Godfrey Kneller, shows Churchill in the robes of Governor of the Hudson's Bay Company.

George Legge, 1st Baron Dartmouth, who although a Protestant, remained loyal to James and commanded the fleet which hoped to intercept William of Orange on his way to England. Portrait after J. Riley, 1685–90.

the overall command remained in the hands of the unpopular but trustworthy Frenchman Feversham. Regiments were summoned from Ireland and Scotland; the land garrisons were strengthened, and men of known loyalty, such as the Duke of Berwick, appointed to command them; while the main body of the army was concentrated at Hounslow to move wherever the invasion might come. James's dispositions seem quite sensible. His main problem was that he did not, of course, know where William would land, and hence was forced to disperse his troops in garrisons round the coast and keep his main army and navy in places from which they might fairly easily be deployed. Most people thought the Prince of Orange would land somewhere on the east coast, probably in Yorkshire; what practically no one could have guessed was that he would sail

186

the whole length of the Channel in November, shepherding his unwieldy collection of transports with his entire naval strength. Anyone who has sailed in the Channel at that time of year will appreciate the risk he took, and one can hardly blame James for expecting him to make the short voyage to Yorkshire.

At last the strong west wind moved a little to the south, and, on 19 October, William was able to get his fleet to sea, the largest ever to engage in an invasion of England. His two or three hundred transports, protected by some fifty fighting ships, carried an army of some thirteen thousand men. In addition to the four thousand English and Scots troops, there were two regiments of mainly English refugees, four of federal Dutch troops paid by the States General, the personal troops of the Prince of Orange, a regiment of French Huguenots, Branden-burgers commanded by James's old companion-in-arms Count Schomberg, now a very old man, and a body of Scandinavian mercenaries, including Marrewis's celebrated dragoons, who were to make a great impression with their blonde hair and black armour. This heterogenous collection of fighting men was given unity by the personality and determination of its commander, in striking contrast to the larger English army which it might expect to meet across the Channel. James's army was already split by quarrels between commanders and, worse still, by the religious prejudices of regimental soldiers who objected to their ranks being filled with Irish papists and command being given to Catholic officers. There were probably more Catholics in William's army than in James's, but there was little religious strife, and the attitude is summed up in the remark made by one of William's Catholic soldiers: 'My soul is God's, but my sword is for the Prince of Orange.' If only James could have inspired such sentiments.

All the same, James seemed to be in luck, and his sailor's instinct right. The day after William set sail, the wind veered again to the west and a storm blew up. William's fleet was dispersed, and, although little damage was done, was forced back to port. James showed little surprise; 'it is not to be wondered at, for the Host has been exposed these several days'. Both he and Dartmouth, who had been much alarmed at the spirit of disloyalty in the English fleet, relaxed, and Dartmouth could write to the King, 'your statesmen may take a nap and recover, the women sleep in their beds, and the cattle, I think, need not be drove from the shore'. William was hardly likely to try again, and by next spring anything could have happened. But this was to underestimate William, always an unwise thing to do. By 1 November, his ships had been re-assembled, horses lost in the storm replaced, and the wind was blowing fair for Yorkshire. The fleet set sail again. On the second night out the wind veered to the east, and, with what seems a sudden change of plan, William ordered the entire armada to sail for the Straits of Dover, passing only fifteen miles from Lord Dartmouth, who, now finding himself on a lee shore, was powerless to do anything. The next morning, the enormous Dutch fleet, dressed overall, fired its cannon in salute as it passed the white cliffs of Dover, and proceeded up the Channel. Could the large crowd of spectators read the words on the Prince of Orange's banner, 'I will maintain the Protestant religion and the liberties of England'? Dartmouth, whose actions were incredibly indecisive throughout the campaign, was left far behind, and William was able to disembark his troops in Torbay, un-challenged from land or sea. He found the ground 'as convenient as could be imagined for the foot in that season'. The date was a notable one, 5 November.

Neither William nor James moved fast after the disembark-ation. William was content to make a dramatic, unchecked entry into Exeter where he made his headquarters. The great army made an enormous impression on the West, and there was virtually no sign of resistance. Leading the troops into Exeter was the Earl of Macclesfield, an ancient Cavalier who had fought for Charles I, at the head of two hundred gentlemen, mostly English, each attended by a negro servant. Perhaps more impressive was the Prince of Orange himself. Although not as pretty as the last invader of the West Country, he was at least much better-looking astride a white charger than standing on his short legs in the council-room. Once installed at Exeter, William established communications with The Hague and with the north, and the cavalry moved forward to cut off the south-west from the rest of the country. William held court, and awaited with confidence the next moves in the game. He wanted his invasion to be bloodless and popular, and had no intention of fighting a savage battle for the crown. While

The imagery contains the following inscriptions: "The Lord Chancellor taken disguisd in Wapping", "Brother Peters what doest thou say —", "Remember ye West", "Remember ym Bishops", "Knock his braines out", "Remember ye mr coote in", "Tear me to peeces.", "Remember magdalen College"

The landing of William of Orange at Torbay was disastrous for Judge Jeffreys, for he had become identified with James's tyrannical methods of government. He attempted to escape disguised as a common seaman, but was recognised at a tavern in Wapping, arrested and taken to the Tower, where he died in April 1689. This contemporary engraving shows the capture of Jeffreys at Wapping.

William waited, matters went as planned. Plymouth was surrendered in his rear; Cheshire and the North, where Danby and others of the signatories of the invitation had great local power, rose in successful revolt; and soon the first trickle of expected deserters from the royal army and from the gentry was making its way to William's camp. There was hardly a sign of enthusiasm for James throughout the country, and before long even his spies were beginning to desert to William. Meanwhile, the royal army stayed at Hounslow waiting for the return of troops sent off to confront the expected invasion of Yorkshire, before slowly moving to camp in Salisbury. James, still trying to

189

Prjntz von Orangen,
Engelandt Año 1689.
D.5 Februarj.

conciliate public opinion, remained in London, lobbied bishops and lords, and promised to call a free Parliament if the Prince of Orange would sail away again. But this was just wishful thinking. James really had only three alternatives – to negotiate with William, to fight, or to run away. He toyed with all three, but, in the end, he chose the last.

This was unfortunately the worst choice. If James had only stayed in the country it seems very unlikely that he would have been deposed. None of the English lords had pledged themselves to make William king – merely to do nothing to oppose his invasion, and, with his assistance, to call a free Parliament to settle the kingdom. Nothing James did could have so played into William's hands as running away. The best course would probably have been to negotiate with the invader. William had no desire to negotiate with James, because this would have compromised his position to operate as an independent arbiter and saviour of the Protestant religion, and because he feared that this would play into the hands of moderates, like Halifax, who had no wish to see him king. He never met James, and did not want to, but, if James had insisted, it would have been difficult for him to refuse. As for fighting, James was a soldier with a reputation for bravery in the field, and he had a considerably larger army than William; so it is difficult to see why he was so reluctant to order an advance into the south-west. One thinks immediately of his remark to the Duke of Buckingham during his career in France. 'I had no mind to expose myself to a certain defeat.' As the tales of treachery poured in from the North, the army and the navy, James must have realised what the likely result of any battle would be. All the same, he decided eventually to advance, as did William, and on 19 November James arrived at Salisbury, while William moved to Axminster, some fifty miles away. But the James who came to Salisbury was not the martial figure of the Battle of the Dunes. Nervous, irresolute and already in despair, he was confined to his room most of the time with a bleeding nose.

While James's nose was bleeding, his world was collapsing about him. In the North the English rebels made themselves masters of Nottingham, York and Hull. Behind him, London was reported to be unquiet. But there was far more dispiriting news from his own camp. Lord Churchill, James's second-in-

James R

Wee doe hereby graciously declare our continued sense of ye long & faythfull services performed to our late dearest Brother & our selfe by Mr. Pepys our Secretary for ye Affayres of our Admiralty of England, & that his long want of Satisfaction to his just pretensions attested by our selfe when Duke of Yorke & confirmed by our sayd dearest Brother in a state thereof beareing date ye second day of March 1678/9 shall bee noe impediment to his receiving ye same from us; wee hereby earnestly recomend-ing him to ye Lords Comiss.rs of our Treasury for theyr doeing him full right on our behalfe therein, & in what is further due to him on his Account as late Treasurer for Tangier. Given at our Castle of Windsor this 17th day of November 1688.

JR

Nov:r 17. 1688.

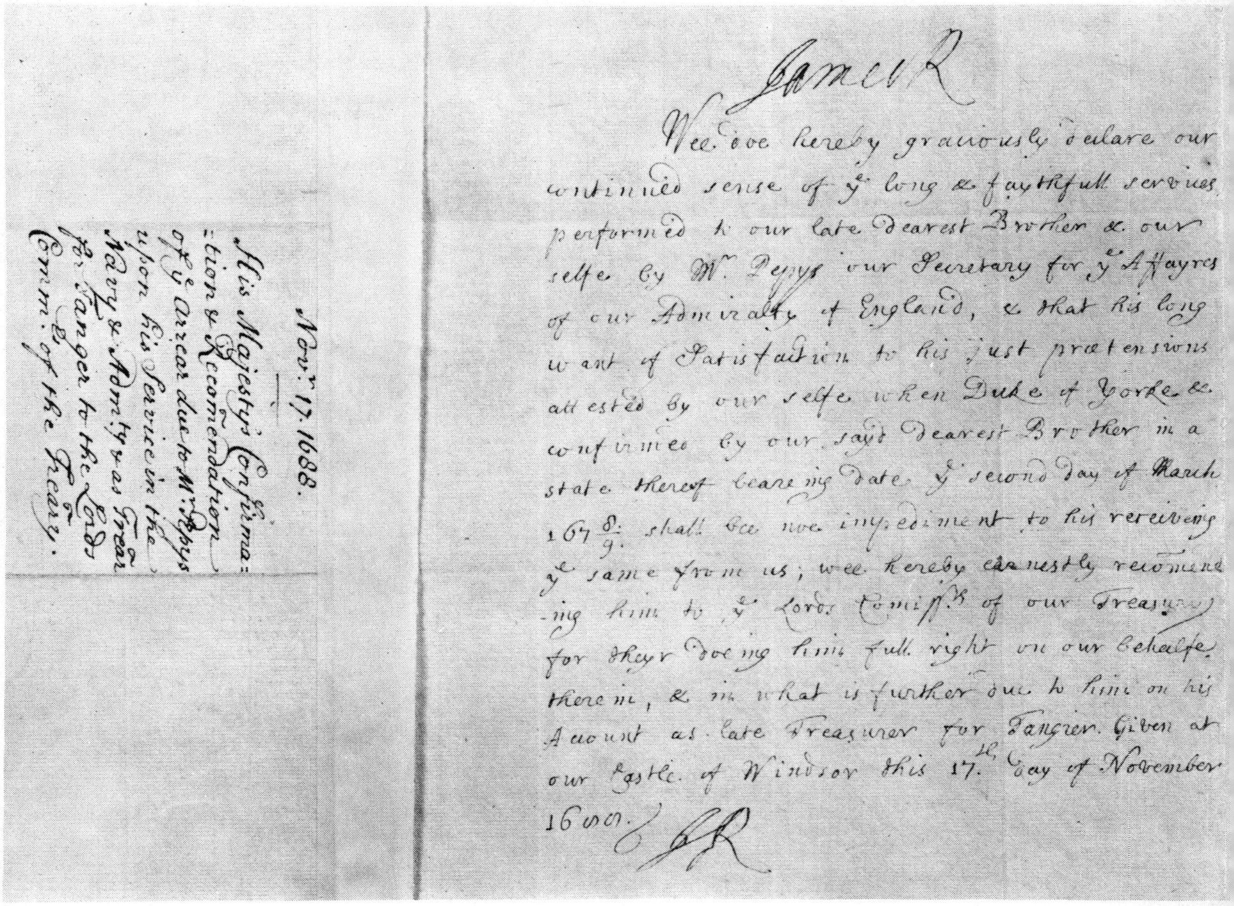

His Majestys Confirma:tion & Recomendation of ye Arrears due to Mr Pepys upon his Service in the Navy & Admiraltyes as Treasr for Tanger to the Lords Comm:rs of the Treasy.

command, who had been in his household for over twenty years, deserted to the enemy, taking with him the Duke of Grafton, one of Charles's bastard sons, many other senior officers and a large contingent of cavalry. This army plot had been long in preparation, and James must have had some inkling of it. Churchill had often claimed that his religion came first with him, but James had never believed that his old friend would desert him in the field, and he was not the only one to be shocked. The despondent James turned back to London without even striking a blow at the invader, only to learn that his own daughter Anne, and her friend Lady Churchill, had left under the escort of the Bishop of London, now divested of his episcopal garments and brandishing a pistol, to join the other

Document written by Samuel Pepys and signed twice by James II, acknowledging the money due to Pepys for his services to the Admiralty and as Treasurer of Tangier. James had left London to meet the invading William of Orange. Pepys accompanied the King as far as Windsor and claimed the sum owing to him – about £28,000. He was never paid.

traitors. It was enough to break any man's heart. For two weeks James wavered, with only the shadow of his former authority left, now deciding to call a Parliament, now determined to negotiate with William, until at last he made his fatal decision. On 12 December, having sent his wife and child before him, he left Whitehall to flee the country, throwing the Great Seal into the Thames on the way. Orders were sent to Feversham directing the army to cease resistance, and to Dartmouth to send those ships still loyal to Ireland, where Tyrconnel retained control. By his desertion, James made up the minds of his people. Scotland declared for the Prince of Orange, but in England, James, by his precipitate flight, left chaos behind him. Feversham did nothing to disband the army, but left it leaderless and unpaid. Bands of discontented soldiers roamed the country to be joined by anti-papist mobs. London called on William to save the country from anarchy.

Poor James! Just as he had forgotten how to fight, so had he forgotten how to flee the country. Father Petre and most of the rest of James's priests, Sunderland, Melfort, the Queen and many others all successfully made their way to France; but not James. Riding through the country roads to avoid capture, he made his way towards the Kent coast, and onto the customs hoy that he had arranged to take him to France. Here James's luck ran out. The hoy went aground on the ebb tide, and James's party was discovered by three boatloads of seamen and fishermen from Faversham searching for fugitives. Their leader, a sword in one hand and a pistol in the other, jumped down into the cabin where James was seated. The King, unrecognised until he was brought back to Faversham, was subjected to some unregal indignities by his capturers, including being searched and abused as a Jesuit. In telling the story, James took a childish pleasure in the fact that he managed to conceal the coronation ring in his drawers. No one, he thought, could replace him as king, so long as he retained this in his possession. Eventually, much to William's annoyance, he was brought back to London. To James's surprise, he was greeted with much joy by the crowds, perhaps saddened to see their King brought so low, but more likely because of the great alarm at the collapse of all order with the King's disappearance.

Back in London, James made the best of matters. He held

The flight of Mary of Modena from Whitehall Palace to France in December 1688.
Unlike her husband's ignominious adventure, Mary's flight was successful.

James departing from Rochester for France, where he landed on Christmas Day 1688.

court, and reassumed the role of king, as if nothing had happened. Lords reappeared to discuss the problems of the kingdom with him, and 'even the papists crept out of their lurking holes'. James's troubles had taught him no tact. Evelyn reports James going to Mass and dining in public, 'a Jesuit saying grace'. But it seems probable that all the time he was determined on a second flight, seeing the only hope of recovering his kingdoms and his prerogative, as he knew it, in fleeing abroad and then re-invading the kingdom from Ireland or from France. He was also clearly frightened of what might happen to him if he fell into William's hands. The concept of William as the second Cromwell was a common one, and James had no wish to share his father's fate. Soon William began to put pressure on him. Dutch guards were sent to replace the loyalists at Whitehall. James in his memoirs says that he was unworried by being surrounded by the Dutch guards and 'went to bed at his usual time, and slept with as much tranquillity as he ever did in his life'. Be that as it may, his tranquillity was rudely disturbed by a deputation who woke him up and demanded that he leave Whitehall 'for the quiet of the city and the safety of his person'. James was much dejected, and asked if it must be done immediately. But he went quietly, only asking if he might go to Rochester, rather than Ham, as had been suggested. William had no objection; indeed he was delighted at James's obvious desire to desert his kingdom, and arranged for a company of Catholic guards from his army to escort him down to Kent. But no guards were left at the back of the house where James was to stay. Disregarding the advice of Middleton and other moderate friends to remain in England, since flight would be interpreted as abdication, James slipped away with his son the Duke of Berwick. He left a paper on his table 'reproaching the nation for their forsaking him'. But, as James's barge took him down the river, it was he who was forsaking his nation. This time his flight was successful, and on Christmas Day 1688 he landed in France. He had lost two kingdoms, his reputation and the people's respect by default. But he still had one kingdom left, and the Catholic wind from Ireland was blowing hard.

8
King over the Water
1689-1701

La Reine d'Angleterre attendant le Roy son Epoux

Mr le Duc de Noaille

Monsieur

WHEN JAMES AND BERWICK slipped away in the yacht *Henrietta*, eating bacon out of an old frying-pan with a hole in it, and no doubt discussing the lack of faith of the English people, a legend had already been born. For nearly sixty years, Jacobite loyalists, some romantic, some simply ambitious, were to plot and scheme and pour out their blood for the sake of the House of Stuart, until at last James's half-Polish grandson, 'Bonnie Prince Charlie', destroyed for ever the hopes of the House on the field of Culloden. The emotions which stirred the London mob to cheer James on his return from Faversham were representative of a nation-wide reaction. Things had gone too far. How could a Tory nation drive out its king? During the complicated process which ended in William and Mary being offered the Crown, there was already a Jacobite party of distressed Tories strongly represented in both Houses of Parliament. The Earl of Arran's reasons for his refusal to recognise William illustrate a common problem faced by many Tories: 'I must distinguish between his Popery and his Person; I dislike the one, but have sworn and do owe allegiance to the other. This makes it impossible for me to concur in an Address which gives the administration of his kingdom to another.' Such people were ineffectual in 1689, but they were to remain a focus of opposition and a potential source of rebellion at least till 1697, plotting and communicating with William's enemies across the sea. Led originally by men like James's brother-in-law, the Earl of Clarendon, and his old friend George Legge, the Jacobite party continued to attract many powerful people, disillusioned by William, to their cause. By 1691, such traditional Royalists as the Duke of Beaufort and the Marquess of Worcester were said by the numerous Jacobite spies to be ready to rise in support of James if he should invade his old kingdom, and even Churchill, now Earl of Marlborough, seemed ready to turn his coat again.

In James's other two kingdoms his position in 1689 seemed even stronger, and it was to be his policy to try to recover his throne through either Ireland or Scotland. The Catholic majority in Ireland, led by Tyrconnel, saw the Revolution as a chance to destroy for ever the Protestant ascendancy in the island. Tyrconnel's systematic replacement of Protestants by Catholics in the civil administration and the army was virtually

200

completed by 1688, and he was now engaged in the last stage of a campaign to destroy the few remaining outposts of Protestant resistance to his rule. But, as James reports in his memoirs, the Protestants in Ulster were 'the most obstinate and bitter enemies he ever had'. Shutting themselves up in the two towns of Londonderry and Enniskillen, the 'mechanic rascals' declared for William, and prepared to endure three grim months of siege by Tyrconnel's troops. The ultimate failure of the Catholic siege of Londonderry, this 'ridiculous siege' as a Jacobite supporter put it, was the beginning of the end of James's Irish hopes, but when he arrived in France at the end of 1688 things looked more than hopeful.

In Scotland, too, he had great hopes. The Presbyterian majority in the northern kingdom, eager once more to throw off the hated bishops, had declared for William; and James's man in Scotland, the Earl of Perth, had been captured and imprisoned. But James had at hand an instrument perfectly designed to inflict a Jacobite revenge on the Presbyterian insurgents. This was John Graham of Claverhouse, Viscount Dundee. Known as 'Butcher Claverhouse' by the Covenanters, for good reasons, but as 'Bonny Dundee' by generations of admiring romantics, he was given a commission by James to raise the Highland clans against the Campbells and the Lowland Presbyterians. The stirring story of the descent of the Highlanders with their claymores on the terrified soldiers sent to fight them in the pass of Killiecrankie has often been told. But victory was won at too great a cost for the Jacobite cause. For Dundee, virtually the only man other than James himself who could have united the clans in a common cause, died of his wounds after the battle, one of the first of a long line of romantic Jacobite martyrs.

> Strike! and when the fight is over,
> If you look in vain for me,
> Where the dead are lying thickest
> Search for him that was Dundee!

After Dundee's death the disunited Highlanders had little success, and soon returned to their normal occupations of fighting each other and stealing the Campbells' cattle.

But James had other potential sources of assistance than his own loyal subjects in Ireland and Scotland. For as soon as William was in power, he declared war on Louis, and thus initiated the struggle that was to involve nearly all Europe till the Peace of Ryswick in 1697. Louis therefore had every reason to want to keep English and Dutch troops pinned down in England or Ireland, and now James was not too proud to refuse his offers of assistance. As soon as he arrived in France, he sought to enlist on his side not only the French, but also the other Catholic powers of Europe. But in this latter ambition James was at least half a century out of date. For William was 'the cement that glues together the different interests of the confederacy', as the Pope himself was to say, and the Catholic powers were not interested in wars of religion, but in assisting their Protestant allies, England, Holland and Prussia, in containing Louis's armies. In France itself, James was much more successful, and was given great assistance by Mary of Modena, who was far more energetic and single-minded than her husband. Much respected in the French Court for her courage and devotion, she had, as that indefatigable letter-writer Madame de Sévigné remarked, 'every appearance, if God willed it, of preferring to

Political cartoon showing Mary of Modena with Louis XIV. Mary proved herself far more energetic in trying to recover the English throne than did James, who became indifferent and seemed content to remain in France.

Let Pleasure Queen, thy Cares remove, Thy Favours too are no defaulters
Thy Loſs of Empire drown'd in Love. To Such a Champion of thy Altars,
Kind Polydorus ſure is worthy, Ioynd against Herdick Causeſo ſtoutt
Thy Smiles, who paid thy Portion for thee. Souls both ſo linkt may kiſs devoutly

reign in the fair kingdom of England, where the Court is large and beautiful, than to remain at St Germain, although overwhelmed with the kindness of the king'.

Louis treated James and Mary with great courtesy, told off some of his courtiers to grace their little Court at St Germain-en-Laye, and provided them with an ample pension to maintain at least some of their regal dignity. But he never in fact engaged in a really massive support of the exiles, despite the obvious attractions of keeping William busy on a second front. Much of the responsibility for this policy of only limited assistance to James rests with Louis's great Minister of War, Louvois, who was always hostile to the expense of an invasion of England, and had a very low opinion of James himself. This opinion was shared by the overwhelming majority of French observers.

James was never the same man after he left England. Whether his physical and mental collapse began at Salisbury or earlier is a matter difficult to ascertain, but he was clearly only a shadow of his former resolute self by the time he arrived in France. An elder generation who remembered the gallant soldier, and everyone who had admired the apparent resolution with which

The Palace of St Germain-en-Laye, which was given to James by Louis for his Court in exile.

Louis XIV with his family and
Madame de Maintenon, by Largillière.
LEFT TO RIGHT Madame de Maintenon,
Duc de Bretagne, the Dauphin, Louis XIV
and Duc de Bourgogne.

he had pushed forward his Catholic policies as king, were very disappointed at the stammering and childish monarch who descended among them. He had even lost that ability to converse fluently in French which had so impressed La Grande Mademoiselle in 1649. Nor did his piety much impress the French Court, who, despite the influence of Madame de Maintenon, were a worldly lot, and were particularly contemptuous of James's obsession with his own salvation and his constant hobnobbing with Jesuits. But perhaps the characteristic most to be derided was his indifference to what happened to him and his lack of determination to recover his throne. He looked 'weary and sadly aged' and he spoke of 'events in England with such a lack of feeling that he inspires little enough for himself'.

James, indeed, despite his appeals for help, seemed quite content to remain quietly in France, hunting with the Dauphin, enjoying the amenities of his own little Court and making occasional trips to enjoy the greater splendour of Versailles. It comes as something of a surprise, after reading the descriptions of him and his way of life, to find that James actually set off to try to recover his kingdoms less than three months after his arrival in France. Louis himself was at Brest to send him off and gave him for his own personal use, his armour, helmet and shield, to bring him luck. And so, in March 1689, he embarked with money, arms for twenty thousand men and a large number of French and refugee officers for Ireland where, according to James, there was 'a great abundance of provisions and men, the loyalest in the world, who are all ready to shed the last drop of their blood in my defence'. Men there were, and prepared to die, but few were soldiers. Tyrconnel had built up an enormous paper army, but his troops were for the most part untrained, unarmed and unpaid. The Protestants, who had fled to Ulster or England, had all the money in Ireland, and there was to be a constant shortage of supplies. Much of the army built up in James's reign had been sent over to England to oppose William. After James's flight, William had wisely rounded up all the Irish soldiers in the English army and had sent them as far away as he could – to assist his ally the Emperor against the Turks on the borders of Hungary. What was left in Ireland were a few good regiments, particularly of cavalry, a few brave and competent leaders from among the Irish gentry, such as Patrick Sarsfield, later Earl of Lucan, and a mass of peasants and wild men from the mountains. Such men were some of the best fighters in Europe, and practically every Catholic king included Irish regiments among the élite of his army, but to be effective against seasoned troops they needed to be trained, and there was neither the time nor the necessary determination to do that in Ireland in 1689.

When James landed at Kinsale on 12 March, he had with him a number of advisers who were not to help in creating the unity necessary for the campaign on which they were engaged. Chief among these were the unpopular and incompetent Melfort and the Comte d'Avaux, an able diplomat sent by Louis to advise James and report back to Versailles on conditions in Ireland. D'Avaux's despatches reveal in great detail both the hopelessness of Tyrconnel's army and the shocking conditions of the whole Irish nation. He was appalled at the prospect of trying to do anything with the material at hand, and reveals prejudices only too common among visitors to Ireland, be they French or English. But, apart from their agreement in condemning the Irish, James and his advisers were agreed on little. In particular, there was a fundamental division of opinion on what the campaign was all about. Melfort and James saw Ireland merely as a stepping-stone to Scotland, and then to England. Tyrconnel wanted an independent Catholic Ireland, supported by French arms and money. And D'Avaux, who saw the Irish campaign solely as a means of forcing William to divert his troops, agreed with Tyrconnel in opposing Melfort's schemes for a landing in Scotland. The division among his advisers made James even more irresolute than he might otherwise have been, and contributed considerably to the failure of the campaign.

But at first things went quite well. James made a great progress from Cork to Dublin, 'the young rural maids weaving of dances before him as he travelled', and entered Dublin to 'loud and joyful acclamations'. Soon a Court had developed round James, and Dublin gave itself up to a somewhat feverish round of gaiety. Officers spent their time in gaming, drinking and whoring, and the city became a centre of vice, condemned by Protestant and Catholic alike. Henry Fitzjames, James's dissolute son by Arabella Churchill, the younger brother of the

206

James's landing at Kinsale in Ireland on 12 March 1689, in his attempt to recover his lost kingdoms.

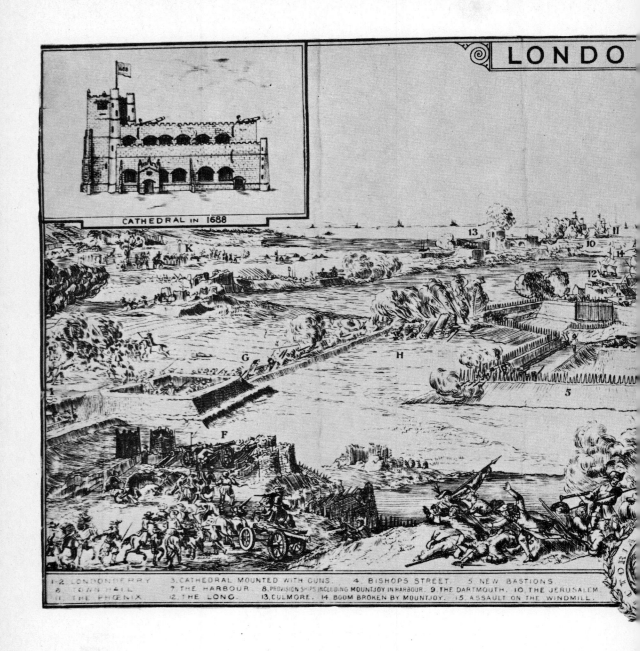

CATHEDRAL in 1688

1·2 LONDONDERRY   3.CATHEDRAL MOUNTED WITH GUNS.   4. BISHOPS STREET.   5 NEW BASTIONS
6. TOWN HALL   7. THE HARBOUR   8. PROVISION SHIPS INCLUDING MOUNTJOY IN HARBOUR. 9. THE DARTMOUTH. 10. THE JERUSALEM
11. THE PHOENIX.   12. THE LONG.   13. CULMORE. 14. BOOM BROKEN BY MOUNTJOY. 15. ASSAULT ON THE WINDMILL.

James's siege of
Londonderry in 1689.
The King and his
French forces are to
be seen at the left.

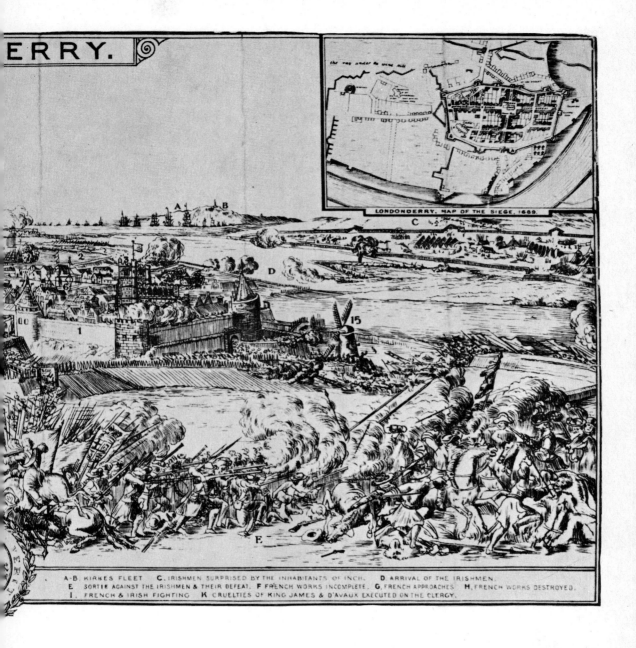

LONDONDERRY, MAP OF THE SIEGE, 1689.

A-B. KIRKES FLEET   C. IRISHMEN SURPRISED BY THE INHABITANTS OF INCH.   D. ARRIVAL OF THE IRISHMEN.
E.   SORTIE AGAINST THE IRISHMEN & THEIR DEFEAT. F. FRENCH WORKS INCOMPLETE. G. FRENCH APPROACHES H. FRENCH WORKS DESTROYED.
I.   FRENCH & IRISH FIGHTING   K. CRUELTIES OF KING JAMES & D'AVAUX EXECUTED ON THE CLERGY.

Duke of Berwick, was among those who set the pace. He was said to be generally too drunk to sit his horse. James did little either to control his officers or to train his army, and the only really positive thing that he did do was to make his way through the desolate and rain-soaked Irish countryside to demand the submission of Londonderry. The reply which he received killed the officer standing at his side, and so 'His Majesty perceiving he was baffled, and his royal dignity affronted' returned to Dublin. Events seemed at last to be moving to some sort of climax when the veteran Schomberg landed in the autumn of 1689, and after some delay James set off with the army from Dublin. But, when he got close to Schomberg, he decided that his old companion-in-arms was too well entrenched to attack, turned round and set off back south to install his army in winter-quarters, while his officers returned to Dublin to enjoy themselves. Schomberg's army, whose well-entrenched position happened to be in a bog, was riddled by disease that winter, and he did no more than James to precipitate any sort of decisive battle. James himself was beset by a fatalistic mood of despair, and Tyrconnel was sure that he would quit the scene at the first check.

Such was the situation when William landed at Carrickfergus with fresh troops in June 1690. James was advised to retire behind the line of the Shannon, and let William tire himself out. But James, in a fit of his old resolution, was determined that 'he would not be walked out of Ireland without at least having one blow for it'. He advanced to the River Boyne, and here at last, on 1 July, uncle and nephew met in battle. A lucky shot seemed to have given the Catholic army and James the confidence they needed to pull them out of their melancholy: William was wounded as he rode forward to reconnoitre. 'This was a thunderbolt to the saints of rebellion, and it was like to put an end to their holy war.' But William lived, and fatalism returned. Rarely can a commander have been more irresolute than James at this final crisis of his career. Not sure whether to fight or retreat, he did nothing either to guard the passes across the river or to put determination into his men, but watched the collapse of his army and his last hope from a hill behind the battlefield. The Irish troops belied the opinion of the French and fought well, particularly the cavalry, but it was a hopeless affair, and

OPPOSITE The Battle of the Boyne, 1 July 1690 – the only pitched battle that took place between James and William. James was forced to watch the collapse of all his hopes from a hill behind the battlefield.

they were soon running, James to Dublin and most of the army to Limerick. William did little to force pursuit, alarmed once again at the prospect of finding James brought in as a prisoner by his over-eager men. But, as Tyrconnel had predicted, James had had enough. Blaming his defeat on the cowardice of his Irish troops, he hardly paused in Dublin on the way to Kinsale, and arrived in France almost as soon as the news of his defeat. The 'cowardly' Irish were to fight bravely for their absent King for another fifteen months before the surrender of Limerick to Schomberg's replacement, the Dutchman Ginkel, ended one more episode in the long struggle for Irish independence. About eleven thousand Irish soldiers were allowed to go to France and engage in Louis's army, and many of them were to share the fate of one of their great leaders, Patrick Sarsfield, who 'now lies the food of crows in Flanders'.

Such is the feeling of doom that overlays this stage of James's career, that it comes as no surprise to learn that he could hardly have chosen a worse date to commit his Irish army to their fate. The day before James lost the Battle of the Boyne, the French Admiral de Tourville won a great victory over the Anglo-Dutch fleet off Beachy Head, and gained complete control of the Channel. With William in Ireland, now, if ever, was the time for that invasion of England which would give James back

A circular horn box reliquary of James II, containing a heart with a smear of blood, a few hairs and a small piece of the Garter ribbon of the King. The piety of James's later years made many accord him the veneration of a saint.

his crown. But Louis, when he heard the news of the Boyne, despaired of James's usefulness, and said that 'it would be so much thrown away to send anything thither'.

Nonetheless, the hopes for the Jacobites were not yet all gone. It was to be another seven years before Louis's recognition of William as King of England ended their schemes to promote a Jacobite rising backed by a French invasion. And less than two years after the Boyne, Louis at last consented to commit ten thousand French troops against England. William was again abroad, the Jacobite party in England was strong, and James had the promise of all the Irish troops in French service. It was once again an optimistic James who made his way to the embarkation camp at La Hougue in the Côtentin peninsula. It was also the same old tactless James who authorised the distribution in England of a manifesto drawn up by Melfort, so damning and so vindictive that the Jacobites in England were compelled to replace it by something rather more likely to attract people to James's colours. While James waited, that Protestant wind from the east, which had done so much to blow away his kingdom, blew again, and delayed the embarkation sufficiently to allow the English under Admiral Russell to sail up and attack the French invasion fleet. The long battle was to reverse the decision of Beachy Head two years previously. As James watched his hopes go up in flames with the French ships, there was a spark of that English pride which had so admired the courage of the Redcoats at the Battle of the Dunes, when he called on his entourage to salute the bravery of the English sailors as they boarded the French ships. He watched the long battle with the professional interest of a sailor, but no one could have guessed from his face that on its outcome depended his future.

The defeat at La Hougue was really the end of James's ambitions to recover his throne. His son the Duke of Berwick said in his memoirs that it was only with the greatest difficulty that James could be distracted from his devotions to take an interest in the next, equally abortive, invasion plan in 1696. For the rest of his life it was to be these devotions that dominated his existence. If God had decided that he would no longer be a king, he would try to be a saint, and, failing that, he would at least do all he could to earn his salvation. James's preoccupation

The children of James II by Mary of Modena. LEFT Louisa Mary, born in exile in 1692 and nicknamed 'his solace' by James. FAR RIGHT James Francis Edward Stuart, the 'Old Pretender'. After James II's death, Mary turned her attentions to trying to restore her son to his rightful patrimony.

with his own salvation was a totally selfish activity, and it is not surprising that, despite his reputation for piety, he never did become a saint. Soon after La Hougue he began his regular visits to the Convent of La Trappe, where the brothers maintained a rule of total silence, except for the cheerful greeting when they met each other – 'We must die, brother; we must die.' Time not spent in such useful occupations as growing vegetables, was spent in contemplating open graves, and they often slept in winding-sheets. Such an atmosphere suited the melancholy and guilt-ridden James to perfection. He wrote to the Abbé de la Trappe, 'you have left the world to work out your salvation; happy are those who can do it, those are the only people I envy'. His trips to La Trappe were interspersed with long periods of fasting, constant prayer, self-imposed penances like wearing an

214

iron chain studded with little sharp points which dug into his skin, and visits to anywhere which had a particularly pious reputation. 'Never was there seen', wrote the Duke of Berwick, 'greater patience, greater tranquillity, or greater joy, than when he thought or spoke of death.'

Needless to say, James in this mood did little to make his small and increasingly crowded Court a place of great gaiety. The Queen, who had a second child in 1692, Louisa Mary, whom James nicknamed his 'Solace', was more cheerful than James, but equally devoted to her priests and pious works, and 'had no taste for gaieties and spectacles'. She was to spend thirty years in exile, much of it engaged in futile attempts to restore first her husband and then her son. She could always find exiles and intriguers interested in such ventures, but in the

1690s most of her courtiers were middle-aged or elderly, and they found little to laugh about. The most distinguished member of James's priest-ridden Court, the Irish soldier and writer Count Anthony Hamilton, who retired to St Germain after the Battle of the Boyne, has left some witty descriptions of the Court and the courtiers: 'The view is enchanting, the works wonderful, and the air so exhilarating that one could make four meals a day, though we have not the wherewithal to provide half that amount.' The best rooms were reserved for the priests who dictated the morals of the courtiers, so that 'agreeable flirtation, even love-making is severely proscribed in this melancholy court'. There could hardly have been a greater contrast with the last English Court in exile.

God had punished James for his sins by taking away his kingdoms. And, even now, God was to make James sweat as he waited for his salvation. Much as James longed for death, he had to wait a long time before it released him from the trials of this world and opened up for him the prospect of eternal salvation. He was still in the hunting field in 1699 at the age of sixty-six. Would his health never give out? But his time was coming, and, at last, in August 1701, he had a stroke when he was hearing Mass, and died three weeks later. During the last fifteen days, when he lay suspended between life and death, he never ceased to hear Mass every day in his room, 'as long as he had force to pray'. The Court crowded round to watch James die like a saint, his face smiling as he comforted his devoted Queen. 'Think of it, Madam', he said, 'I am going to be happy.'

Let us hope that James did find happiness in death, for he was dismal enough in life. Except for his military career in France, and the short period of dissolute glory in the first five years of the Restoration, his life had been for the most part a record of failure and disappointment. It is true that he brought his own troubles upon himself. In a cynical age, it is easy enough to sneer at the mysteries of conversion and to assume that all religious men are hypocrites. But James was no hypocrite. The sincerity of his conversion rings through everything he did, and his failure, for failure he certainly was, is on the grand scale. For James was a man who thought that he had seen the truth, and knew that, once having seen it, his duty lay in trying to lead five million men and women to their salvation. He failed because men prefer to find the truth for themselves rather than be forced to see it. He failed, too, because in the end he found himself not to be the man of courage and resolution that he and others thought he was. James blames his ultimate failure on his own sins, particularly that besetting sin of incontinence which pervades his life. Many contemporaries and modern historians interpret James's interpretation in a less spiritual way, and suggest that the reason for James's breakdown in his last years was the long-term effect of venereal disease. Was James, then, just another syphilitic king? Historians love to explain the inconsistencies of kings by their vices. It is an easy way out, since there is no possibility of proof. But do we need to use such an explanation? Syphilitic he may have been, but surely there are few men who could have faced the betrayals that James faced at Salisbury, and later, without breaking down. Ever since his conversion he had known unpopularity and stubborn resistance, but he had always had a coterie of friends. When these disappeared James's world collapsed. But James's world had been collapsing long before Salisbury. His trouble was that he was not sufficiently aware of the world to realise it. For the man whom Coleman had described as being 'zealous of being the author and instrument' of the glorious work of leading England back to Rome, was a fool, and lacked any sense of political reality. One of the best descriptions of him comes from a great lady of the French Court in the 1690s: 'To tell the truth, our good King James is a brave and honest man, but the silliest I have ever seen in my life; a child of seven would not make such crass mistakes as he does. Piety makes people outrageously stupid.' Piety, not syphilis, was James's disease.

'Our good King James is a brave and honest man, but the silliest I have ever seen in my life'

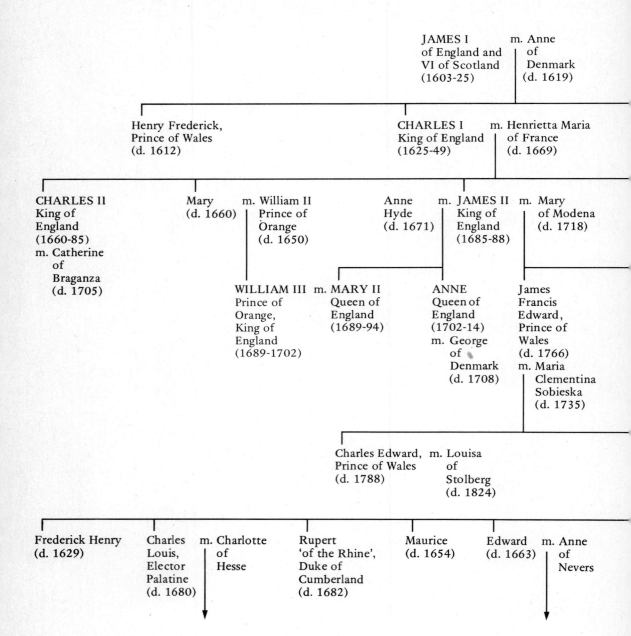

JAMES I
of England and
VI of Scotland
(1603-25)

m. Anne
of
Denmark
(d. 1619)

Henry Frederick,
Prince of Wales
(d. 1612)

CHARLES I
King of England
(1625-49)

m. Henrietta Maria
of France
(d. 1669)

CHARLES II
King of
England
(1660-85)
m. Catherine
of
Braganza
(d. 1705)

Mary
(d. 1660)

m. William II
Prince of
Orange
(d. 1650)

Anne
Hyde
(d. 1671)

m. JAMES II
King of
England
(1685-88)

m. Mary
of Modena
(d. 1718)

WILLIAM III
Prince of
Orange,
King of
England
(1689-1702)

m. MARY II
Queen of
England
(1689-94)

ANNE
Queen of
England
(1702-14)
m. George
of
Denmark
(d. 1708)

James
Francis
Edward,
Prince of
Wales
(d. 1766)
m. Maria
Clementina
Sobieska
(d. 1735)

Charles Edward,
Prince of Wales
(d. 1788)

m. Louisa
of
Stolberg
(d. 1824)

Frederick Henry
(d. 1629)

Charles
Louis,
Elector
Palatine
(d. 1680)

m. Charlotte
of
Hesse

Rupert
'of the Rhine',
Duke of
Cumberland
(d. 1682)

Maurice
(d. 1654)

Edward
(d. 1663)

m. Anne
of
Nevers

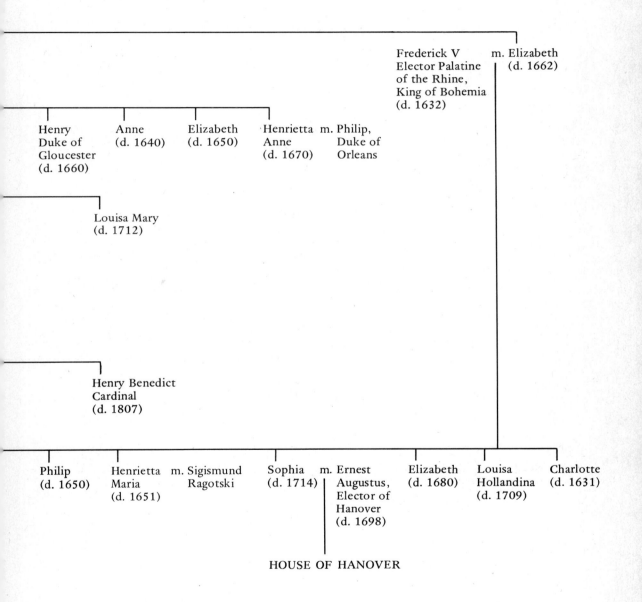

Frederick V
Elector Palatine
of the Rhine,
King of Bohemia
(d. 1632)   m. Elizabeth
                      (d. 1662)

Henry   Anne   Elizabeth   Henrietta m. Philip,
Duke of   (d. 1640)   (d. 1650)   Anne   Duke of
Gloucester   (d. 1670)   Orleans
(d. 1660)

Louisa Mary
(d. 1712)

Henry Benedict
Cardinal
(d. 1807)

Philip   Henrietta m. Sigismund   Sophia   m. Ernest   Elizabeth   Louisa   Charlotte
(d. 1650)   Maria   Ragotski   (d. 1714)   Augustus,   (d. 1680)   Hollandina   (d. 1631)
                (d. 1651)   Elector of   (d. 1709)
                                                         Hanover
                                                         (d. 1698)

HOUSE OF HANOVER

Select bibliography

The best full-length biography of James II is by F. C. Turner (1948). Two interesting shorter biographies are by Hilaire Belloc (1928) and F. M. G. Higham (1934).

The period of James's life has attracted many historians, but T. B. Macaulay's *History of England* remains a brilliant study. The first two volumes cover James's lifetime. For those who object to Macaulay's Whig bias, two volumes by David Ogg give perhaps the fairest view of the period. They are *England in the Reign of Charles II* and *England in the Reigns of James II and William III*.

The second half of the seventeenth century abounds in diaries and memoirs. Madame de Motteville's memoirs of the Court of Anne of Austria, Anthony Hamilton's memoirs of the Comte de Grammont and the diaries of Pepys and Evelyn are those which I found most useful. To these might be added Bishop Burnet's *History of his Own Time*, which is a combination of history and memoir.

There are excellent biographies of many of the individuals who played a prominent part in James's life. In particular, I would mention the first two volumes of W. S. Churchill, *Marlborough, his life and times*; K. H. D. Haley, *The First Earl of Shaftesbury*; J. P. Kenyon, *Robert Spencer, Earl of Sunderland* and Carola Oman, *Mary of Modena*.

Books covering particular episodes in James's life include Charles Wilson, *Profit and Power*, about the Dutch Wars; Sir John Pollock, *The Popish Plot*; J. R. Jones, *The First Whigs*, about the Exclusion Crisis; Maurice Ashley, *The Glorious Revolution of 1688* and John Carswell, *The Descent on England*, about William's invasion; E. & M. S. Grew, *The English Court in Exile*, on the Jacobite Court at St Germain-en-Laye.

Finally, one book fundamental in understanding James is the edition by Godfrey Davies of the *Papers of Devotion of James II*.

Index